A Kitchen on Goose Cove

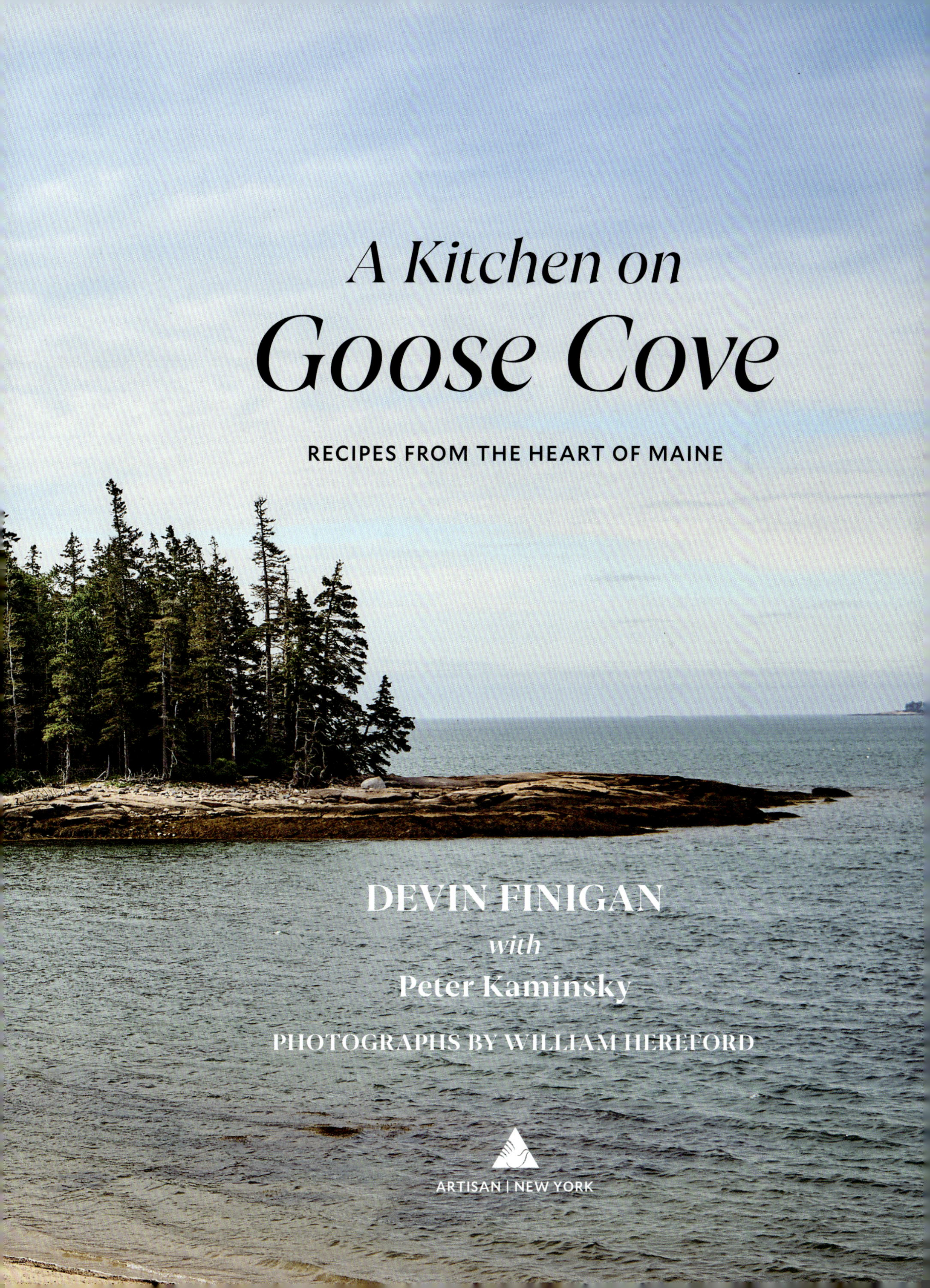

A Kitchen on Goose Cove

RECIPES FROM THE HEART OF MAINE

DEVIN FINIGAN

with

Peter Kaminsky

PHOTOGRAPHS BY WILLIAM HEREFORD

ARTISAN | NEW YORK

Library of Congress Cataloging-in-Publication Data is on file.

ISBN 978-1-64829-407-5 (hardcover)
ISBN 978-1-64829-409-9 (ebook)

Design by Suet Chong

Published by Artisan
an imprint of Workman Publishing,
a division of Hachette Book Group, Inc.
1290 Avenue of the Americas
New York, NY 10104
artisanbooks.com

Printed in China (APO) on responsibly sourced paper

First printing, March 2026

10 9 8 7 6 5 4 3 2 1

for

Annabel Lee

and

Emmylou Wilde

CONTENTS

Foreword

The midcoast of Maine is one of the most beautifully rugged, yet naturally refined places you will ever find . . . *anywhere.* It's where sea and pine are uniquely inseparable and dance in a harmony that stirs and inspires both heart and mind. The coastline is dotted with so many islands, coves, and harbors that it's impossible not to get lost in exploration and discovery every time you take a winding drive along the coastal backroads or meander by boat through countless pristine waterways. Known all over for its exceptional maritime culture, fresh and abundant seafood, and giving rise to some of the best restaurants in the world, Maine is quite simply an impressive natural resource for unbelievable food, extraordinarily resourceful people, and amazing life experiences.

But it takes a special person to choose to make their life here. And more special still, to build a restaurant here. The winters are long, cold, and harsh. And the short, make-or-break, summer high seasons in the restaurant business bring all the challenges of living and dying by the seasonalities of weather, ingredients, and staffing. To live and thrive in Maine year-round takes an unwavering, deep-seated commitment along with grit, heart, passion, and a clear vision for making it all happen. And Devin Finigan embodies all of that and so much more . . . taking her work and commitment to her farmers, foragers, and fisherman with absolute seriousness . . . and yet, at the same time, without taking herself too seriously at all. She is a romantic. She knows how to have fun. She always stays grounded, humble, honest, and hardworking while continuously striving to be her very best . . . bringing warmth and romance to every plate she serves and the spaces she creates.

I remember seeing Devin one Sunday morning years ago on the deck of her first restaurant in Stonington, Maine, as she glided with purpose through the buzz and bustle of a busy brunch service. She didn't really know who I was at the time, but I watched quietly as she expertly broke down a freshly caught halibut right there on the side deck, all while carrying her baby on her back. She was doing the impossible—deftly balancing all the forces at play in that moment—place, people, profession, and all the priorities that come with being a mother. Her business, her baby, and that giant fish all gracefully, peacefully, intentionally held in orbit around her. It was truly inspiring.

Then in the spring of 2019, I received a note from Devin asking to meet with me. She wanted some advice on how to define and build the type of restaurant that would draw people in from everywhere. The kind of destination experience whose reputation would be its lifeblood. She was clearly set on making a big move from her original little place in Stonington, and I was impressed by her energy and motivation. Her eyes sparkled as she gushed poetically, speaking a mile a minute, painting for me the vision in her mind . . . the romantic candlelit dining room washed in hues of rose and celadon . . . the sounds of lapping waves on the nearby shoreline and a foghorn in the distance . . . the lobster boats and sailboats drifting silently along the horizon on their way to Stonington Harbor . . . and the smell of briny breezes mixing with the scent of beach roses on warm summer evenings. I was transported there as she spoke. And this singular vision of a magical destination is what Devin has created, and it's where she has arrived. Aragosta at Goose Cove, Deer Isle, Maine. Here she is home, literally and figuratively. Her dream actualized, she is exactly where she should be: serving food that is as stunning as the south-facing view out into the Penobscot Bay that comes with every meal.

Devin knows the magic that comes from fearlessly committing to a place, purpose, and the people around you. She knows the power that comes from pouring love into everything you do. She knows the strength she has gained simply by committing to her craft . . . a craft in which she creates, serves, and cares for others with every ounce of her being. Giving them her complete heart on a plate in the place she calls home. It's all so palpable without being overly earnest. Her love can be felt. You can taste it. And that is what makes Devin and her beautiful Aragosta so undeniable.

This book . . . *her* book . . . is your beautifully compelling passport straight to the heart of what she does best. In these pages, Devin has distilled down for us all her years of extremely hard work, relentless trial and error, and world-class culinary invention and creativity into a guide for how to feed people with romance and memorable experiences through unbelievably beautiful and inspired dishes.

—Erin French

The Magic of Maine

My home is on Deer Isle, Maine, a rocky, forested island in Penobscot Bay. It connects to the mainland by a slender bridge over a wide channel known as Eggemoggin Reach. My two daughters and I share our house with a pair of friendly bulldogs who will sometimes interrupt their naps to give a lazy woof when visitors stop by. We live at the end of an unpaved road that winds through a deep forest of spruce carpeted with wild mushrooms, caribou moss, and sunlit patches of lowbush blueberries. Except for the more populated summer months, white-tailed deer and wild turkey are more common sights than people. From our vantage point on high ground, we look out on the curving arc of Goose Cove. Its sandy beach is ringed by grassy dunes and a necklace of beach roses and wild mustard. From time to time, a long white furrow, left behind by a lobster boat, etches its path on the smooth surface of the sea. It's a very easy place to daydream.

You could say my love affair with Maine was a case of love at first sight *and* scent. Like so many others, I was hooked from the first visit. I wasn't born here, but I feel I was born to be here.

Maine's beauty and spirit are bewitching. I'm drawn to the cool clean scent of the evergreen forest and the briny aroma of sea mist rolling off Penobscot Bay. I love the neat white houses straight out of a painting from another century, the random stacks of lobster traps piled up by a salt-splotched pickup truck in a fisherman's front yard, the daylilies along the roadside, and the old-timey farm stands with their wooden crates and bushel baskets overflowing with the bounty of the season.

The stirrings of early spring, when you can hear the sun-splashed *drip drip* of ice melting off the rocky ledges in the first warm days of April, are a sign of hope and renewal. After that we get a parade of wildflowers and pastel green leaves as spring bursts out, and then the strawberries of June, and the sweet corn that seems to grow six inches every day in July, and the lowbush blueberries and ripe peaches of August. And then the fall! There never was a season on earth that blazes with flaming color like an autumn in Maine. Even in winter, huddled around the woodstove, watching the steel-gray sea and listening for the low moan of buoys rocked by the tides, Maine has its homey charms. And through all the seasons, there's the hum of diesel engines as fishing boats harvest the bountiful gifts of the sea.

My Journey

When I was young, Maine was a place that my family visited for a few weeks every summer from our home in Vermont. We lived on a country road in the Green Mountains: my dad, my mom, my three sisters, a milk cow named Flower, and Candy, our brown-and-white pony. Our two acres were always a work in progress. My dad's ongoing project was building flower beds and bluestone walls in the classic New England style. My mom, who was a nurse, also worked at the local farm stand. We always had plenty of whatever vegetables were in season. I was eager to help out tending to the flowers, lugging bluestone, stacking lots of firewood, and helping my mom put up canned vegetables or create wreaths and decorations for Halloween, Thanksgiving, and Christmas.

My dad was a sous-chef at the Inn at Sawmill Farm, a fine-dining restaurant in the heart of ski country. It catered to a seasonal crowd that wanted gourmet food but also some local tradition (a formula that I would follow years later when I opened Aragosta, my own restaurant). I earned extra money all through high school working at the Sawmill and I grew to love the clatter and clang of a restaurant kitchen running on all cylinders. Cooking became a second language that I learned just by being around it so much.

I didn't plan on opening a restaurant when I made a right turn off Route 1. I didn't have much of a plan for anything: I was nineteen, and just recovered from blowing out my knee, which had put an end to any fantasies of pursuing a snowboarding career. My sister, Melanie, had come to Deer Isle

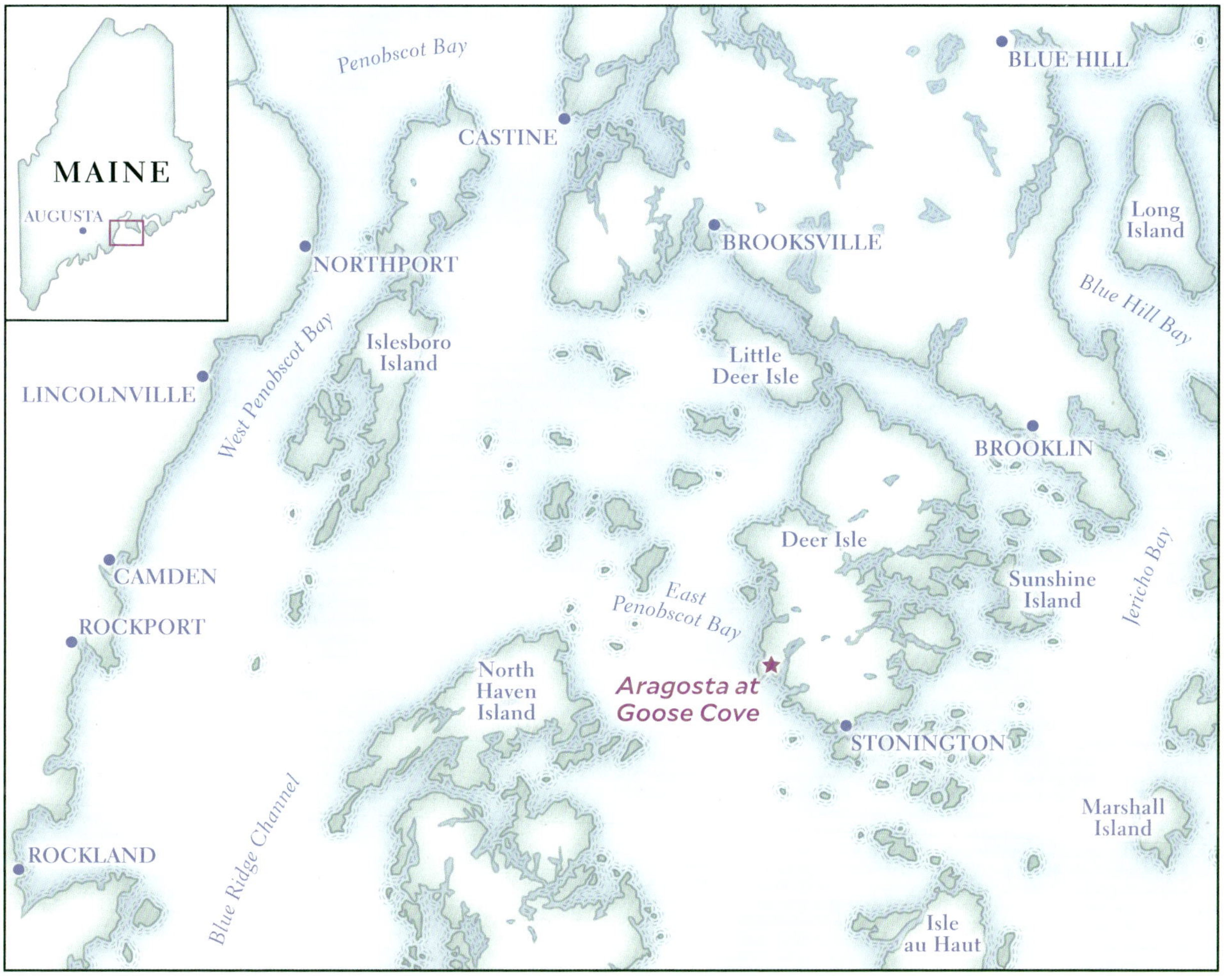

for a session at the Haystack Mountain School of Crafts, where generations of artisan weavers, woodworkers, and ceramicists have created an arts scene alongside Deer Isle's ancient fishing community. Arts and crafts, and fishing, and young people who did all three—that was the Deer Isle scene, and it fit me to a T. So, after a year of art school in Savannah, I decided Maine was where I wanted to be and I've never looked back.

Here to Stay

Maine had a hold on me that wouldn't let go, and like the generations before me seeking a life of small towns and villages where life was lived at nature's pace, I put together a patchwork of jobs that made it possible for me to put down roots, raise a family, and build a life as a Mainer. In those early years, I took whatever gigs I could find. I pounded nails on construction sites, shingled roofs, crewed on a sailboat, flipped pancakes, baked blueberry muffins, shucked oysters, and stuffed lobster rolls. Drawing on my years of gardening with my parents, I found work taking care of the gardens of the summer people and caretaking for their properties in the offseason. I bicycled to my jobs because I didn't own a car yet. My bike had a baby seat where I would bungee-cord a cooler with my lunch and some cold drinks.

In those early years, I worked my way up the restaurant ladder from breakfast cook to line cook, to chef at an upscale inn, to my own restaurant on the harbor in Stonington, the world's biggest lobster port. It was a blessing of sorts that restaurant work was so seasonal. It gave me the opportunity to travel and learn new cooking skills in the offseason. For four years, I went to Italy on monthlong trips where I cooked for American tourists who lodged at a Tuscan farmhouse in the village of Castellina in Chianti. I learned so much about pasta and prime ingredients in Italy. When it came time to give a name to my own restaurant, my ex-husband, Luke, suggested that I combine my love of Italian cooking with coastal Maine's iconic dish.

"What's the Italian word for *lobster*?" he asked.

"Aragosta," I said.

Aragosta's first incarnation in Stonington was a hit. It also taught me that if I was going to be as successful as a mom, commuting an hour every day to a restaurant, expediting orders while pregnant (I did that twice), and pumping breast milk between shifts was not the ideal way to raise children. Then fate lent a hand: An old roadhouse with some guest cottages at the end of a dirt road became available. It had been a well-respected restaurant that once served Julia Child a dinner that featured carrot risotto. By the time I found out about the property, though, it had fallen on hard times: It was more of a watering hole for Stonington's fishermen than a real restaurant. (There's a local saying that "Stonington is a drinking town with a fishing problem.") I could see great potential: Situated on twenty-one acres with a breathtaking view of Penobscot Bay, there was a main lodge, a bunch of guest cabins, and one winterized cabin where my family could live while we built a house, a short walk from the lodge. It was a pretty ideal setup for a chef-mom.

The people who come to Aragosta want modern food and new recipes that carry the taste of Maine. I've worked, learned, and picked up ideas in some of the world's great restaurants: Per Se and Blue Hill in New York City,

SingleThread in California wine country, El Jardín on Mallorca, and Verjus in Paris. You could say the cuisine that grew out of those experiences is my own mash-up of all those travels and the bounty of Maine.

Japanese and Korean ingredients have also had a big influence on my cooking. This shouldn't be surprising. After all, the waters of Goose Cove, and all along the coast of Maine, are cold and teeming with life. Halfway around the world, the waters of the Sea of Japan and the northern Pacific are similarly chilly and rich with the same sea life. Maine has quite naturally adopted many ingredients from those distant seas.

For nearly half the year, when Aragosta's season ends, I'm a home cook for family and friends. I make long-cooked stews using Maine ingredients like littlenecks and cod, spur-of-the-moment one-dish meals, Maine's famous whoopie pies for after-school snacks, and family projects like pot stickers (that come out best when pinched together by my daughters' hands). Every year in apple-picking time I invite friends to a cider press on the beach, build a roaring fire, and make my version of spareribs, baked beans, and pies that wouldn't be out of place at a tailgate party. Any time of year when the beach beckons for food and fire, I jump at the chance.

For any cook who wants to bring changes to old New England favorites or try out new dishes incorporating the global food conversation, it is a *very* good time to be in Maine. Our organic farmers have cracked the code for the most intensely flavorful vegetables. Our local fishermen bring in halibut, cod, haddock, hake, mackerel, and giant bluefin tuna. Our lobster fishers pull in traps full of the sweetest lobsters. A new generation of oyster farmers is raising bushels of briny oysters; learning from them, I've started to raise oysters as well. My favorite scalloper went to Japan, where he learned how to raise scallops in the wild without having to disturb the sea floor. Foraging in the forests, fields, and meadows, we are blessed with mushrooms, berries, ramps, and fiddlehead ferns. From the shallows of Penobscot Bay, we gather umami-rich seaweeds washed up by the tides. As regular as a ticking grandfather's clock, they lap against the shore of my island home. It is a privilege to share it all with you and convey the feel and the flavors of the heart of Maine.

My Main Ingredients

Maine is a vast state. Our forests, fields, and farms provide us with a cornucopia of seasonal ingredients. Our tidal flats and deeper offshore waters offer up a never-ending procession of seafood changing with the seasons. Although some of these ingredients might be available in your home area, too, I'll also give you a list of my Maine purveyors that offer the same ingredients that I use every day (see Resources, page 318).

From the Waters

Brook trout: Known as "salters" because they migrate from the ocean into our streams in early May, our unique sea-run brookies are pink-fleshed like salmon. In the interest of conservation, I let them go and use farm-raised brookies. But eating one or two a year is a special treat.

Clams: Steamers, littlenecks, and quahogs nestle in the tidal flats up and down the coast. I use both the flesh and the brine in recipes.

Cod: White-fleshed, flaky, and mild tasting, cod has been a mainstay of Maine cuisine for centuries in chowders, fish cakes, and fish and chips.

Haddock: This less costly but equally flaky cousin of cod is a Maine favorite that works in any cod recipe.

Halibut: We have a short halibut season each May, and when the first halibut of the year is reeled in, I take it as a sure sign that spring is here to stay.

Lobster: The Gulf of Maine is the world's most productive lobster fishery, and lobster is the first thing that comes to mind when folks think of Maine foods.

Mackerel: They swarm around Deer Isle in late spring and early autumn. Quickly fried, grilled over hot coals, or smoked, they are deeply flavorful.

Mussels: Plump and tender mussels are harvested and farm-raised along the entire coast of Maine.

Oysters: Our rocky inlets are prime habitat for plump briny oysters.

Peekytoe crabs: These newcomers to Maine waters have become a favorite of chefs all over America.

Scallops: The waters around Deer Isle abound in sweet scallops.

Tuna: Although they usually range farther out to sea, every year some lucky fisherman catches one of these giant fish, and there is sushi, sashimi, and pan-seared tuna steaks galore.

From Forest, Field, and Shore

Apple cider: In the fall, about the time that all our broad-leaved trees start to blaze with color, I set up a cider press on the beach, make a party of it (see pages 86–87), and press gallons of fresh cider.

Chanterelles: Wild mushroom gatherers reap a generous harvest after a summer rain when sunlight warms the forest floor. We also have black trumpets, some morels, and shaggy manes.

Fiddlehead ferns: Another early-spring foraged green, fiddleheads are crispy and fresh-tasting, great for pickling or sautéing in butter as a side or for topping fresh fish.

Grains: Our hearty local wheat is well adapted to Maine's climate and soil; I use its flour in recipes that call for all-purpose flour, including Maine's signature Anadama Bread (page 179). We also have a special Black Nile barley that has a nutty flavor and deep brown/black color. Maine produces great buckwheat, which, although not technically a grain, adds similar toasty flavor to breads, griddle cakes, and cookies.

Maple syrup: I wait with anticipation for sugaring time each year during the last part of winter when the sap starts to rise in our gorgeous maples. I often use syrup in place of sugar to give a sweet local accent to desserts.

Ramps: These wild cousins of scallions and garlic grow along riverbanks and we harvest them in late April through mid-May. They are quite sharp and are lovely sautéed, in braises, or pickled.

Spruce tips: When spring begins, Maine forests reawaken and the spruce trees grow tender pale green

buds that give a fresh, bright accent to fruit ices and rice dishes.

Sugar kelp and dulse: We forage these edible seaweeds in the shallows along our shores. They add flavor-boosting umami that pumps up the savoriness of stews, braises, and poaching liquids. You can use them as dry flakes as well.

Wild blueberries: Our lowbush wild blueberries are potent flavor packages that shout "It's summer in Maine!"

Wild mustard seeds: The tiny, bright yellow flowers of wild mustard grow all over the dunes along Goose Cove. The pickled seeds are wonderful as a garnish or as part of the mix for Refrigerator Pickles (page 311).

Wild strawberries: In the first part of June, these little ruby jewels grow along sunlit patches of the forest. They are easy to pick and easy to eat, too, so take care to not eat them all before making a recipe.

From Around the Globe

My larder is stocked with ingredients from Maine but also from many far-flung sources from Japan to Italy. Here are the ones that I cook with the most.

Dukkah: A mix of nuts and seeds from North Africa that lends crunch and notes of aromatic spice; used as a finishing garnish.

Espelette pepper: A mildly spicy, slightly sweet chile pepper from the Basque region of France. You can substitute red pepper flakes, which are more commonly available.

Fermented black beans: Fermented black soybeans are rich in umami, salt, and a bit of tanginess. In contrast to most dried beans—which tend to fade into the background—their flavor really stands out.

Furikake: A crunchy, salty, sweet, umami-rich Japanese condiment. It is often served on sushi or to give a crunchy flavorful finish to many Japanese recipes.

Harissa: A spice paste that adds mild heat, aromatic notes, and a bit of tanginess that brightens the flavors of stews and sauces.

Hijiki: A seaweed that grows along rocky shores and is gathered at low tide and then dried. If you've ever had a seaweed salad at a sushi bar, the crunchy, salty vegetable that looks like dark-colored linguine is hijiki.

Kimchi: Think Korean sauerkraut—a funky, spicy, fermented cabbage dish that can complement the strongest, richest flavors.

Kombu: Also known as sugar kelp or devil's apron. We find it everywhere by the seaside. It grows particularly well along the mooring lines of boats and is super high in umami. If you don't live near the sea, kombu is available in dried sheets.

Mirin: A mildly sweet, low-alcohol rice wine. Used in sauces to balance flavor in the same way that a medium sherry, like amontillado, works in Spanish sauces.

Nori: The literal translation from Japanese is "sea moss." It is a form of dried algae that is used to wrap sushi. In Wales and Scotland, it is also known as laver. It has some subtle sharp notes that help focus flavor.

Ponzu: A tart, salty, sweet, umami-rich sauce. It often includes soy sauce, mirin, yuzu, and kombu. Just as with American barbecue sauces, different cooks have their own mix of ingredients.

Preserved lemon: A staple of Arab cuisine, salted, long-cured lemon adds intensely bright and salty notes to stews, sauces, and salads.

Rice vinegar: Made from fermented rice, it is mildly tangy.

Saffron: Harvested and processed by hand, saffron threads are picked from the heart of a particular crocus. It is famously expensive, which is why home cooks often steer clear of it, but, in fact, the amount called for in most recipes is quite economical. It's particularly good with seafood.

Thai fish sauce: Umami + funk, this sauce is made with fermented anchovies packed in sea salt. Italian chefs (or anybody who cooks Italian food) will recognize its similarity to colatura di alici (Italian fish sauce made from anchovies). It's very fishy and I love that.

Yuzu: A citrus fruit that tastes kind of like lemon and grapefruit, tangy and bitter all at once. It is an important ingredient in such multiflavored condiments as ponzu (see left), but it is also nice all on its own as a finishing touch on seafood.

LOBSTER

If you walk along Stonington Harbor or any other wharf dotting the Maine coast, don't expect to see fancy yachts or expensive sailboats; the harbor will be filled with the workboats of men and women who make their living on the sea, most of them going for lobsters. Maine is the biggest lobster producer in the world, and Stonington, on Deer Isle, is the world's largest lobster port. The cold, relatively shallow waters of Penobscot Bay are pretty near to paradise if you happen to be a lobster. Lobstering is a tough way to make a living—out on the water in early morning, baiting and pulling traps in all kinds of weather short of a hurricane or a roaring nor'easter. And lobster fishers work nearly all year round, even in wintry seas. They are a tough, independent breed who work for themselves in natural surroundings that can be heavenly one day and horrific the next. When you get your hands on the legendary shellfish, you relish it. Try the Lobster Rolls (page 30), which are easier than you think to make at home, or Lobstah & Pastah (page 46) for a meal that is simple yet luxurious.

LOBSTER ROLLS

The first thing that visitors typically seek as soon as they cross over the New Hampshire/Maine line is a lobster roll—usually a quarter pound of lobster meat, dressed with lemon, butter, and mayo (or all three) and stuffed into a buttered and toasted split-top bun. It's an icon of Maine cuisine. Here you'll dress chunks of lobster with a made-from-scratch aioli, amped up with brown butter and miso.

MAKES 6 ROLLS

- 1½ pounds (680 g) cooked lobster meat (see How to Steam a Lobster, page 32; also, see Note)
- ¼ cup (60 g) Miso Brown Butter Aioli (page 308)
- 1 celery rib, medium-diced
- 1 medium shallot, finely diced
- 1 tablespoon fresh lemon juice
- 4 tablespoons (60 g/½ stick) unsalted butter, at room temperature
- 6 split-top buns
- ¼ cup (8 g) fresh flat-leaf parsley leaves, for garnish
- 1 lemon, cut into 6 wedges

1. In a medium bowl, combine the lobster, aioli, celery, and shallot. Toss gently to coat the meat. The lobster should be lightly coated but not weighed down with aioli. Taste the mixture and adjust with the lemon juice for brightness.

2. Melt the butter in a cast-iron skillet over medium heat. Toast the buns until golden brown on both sides, 1 to 2 minutes.

3. To assemble, divide the lobster mixture evenly among the buns. Garnish with the parsley and serve with lemon wedges alongside for squeezing.

NOTE: A mix of knuckle and claw lobster meat makes the juiciest and most tender mix. You can order it direct from Stonington's own Greenhead Lobster (see Resources, page 318); it's as economical as cooking whole lobsters.

HOW TO STEAM A LOBSTER

There are many ways to cook a lobster. You can boil it or bake it or grill it over a charcoal fire, but for foolproof, no-fuss lobster cooking, steaming it is quick and easy.

In a pot large enough to comfortably hold the lobsters, bring a few inches of liberally salted water to a boil over high heat. Place the live lobsters in the pot and cover with the pot lid. Steam the lobsters until they are cooked through. A standard 1½-pound (680 g) lobster will take around 12 minutes. A 2-pound (900 g) lobster will take 18 to 20 minutes. You'll know a lobster is cooked when one of its whiskers (antenna) detaches easily when pulled. You can serve the lobsters in their shells or, if you are using the meat for another recipe, crack the shells when they are cool enough to handle and remove the meat (see How to Break Down a Lobster, page 44). Save the heads and shells for Tidal Broth (page 304).

Note that you can also buy lobster meat, cooked or uncooked (see Resources, page 318). Sometimes buying the lobster meat is the most convenient way to go, though you won't have any shells left over to make broth.

SMOKED CREAM LOBSTER BISQUE

Although lobster is the basis for many classic Maine summertime meals, cold rainy weather, brisk autumn days, or freezing winter afternoons feel warmer and cozier with a rich, savory bisque. Lobster is not an inexpensive ingredient, but this bisque lets you serve up to 8 people with the meat of just 2 or 3 lobsters. Tidal Broth, thickened with a roux, gives this bisque a full-on artillery blast of flavor with a smooth, velvety body reinforced by the richness of the smoked cream.

SERVES 8 AS A MAIN COURSE

- 2 quarts (1.92 L) Tidal Broth (page 304) or store-bought lobster stock
- 2 cups (480 ml) smoked cream (see How to Smoke Cream, page 36)
- 4 tablespoons (60 g/½ stick) unsalted butter
- ¼ cup (30 g) all-purpose flour
- 12 ounces (340 g) cooked lobster meat (see How to Steam a Lobster, page 32)
- Grated zest and juice of 1 lemon
- 1 tablespoon sherry vinegar
- Kosher salt
- 2 to 3 tablespoons fresh tarragon leaves

1. In a soup pot, combine the broth and smoked cream and bring to a simmer over medium heat.

2. Meanwhile, warm the butter in a small saucepan over medium heat until it begins to foam. Whisk in the flour a little bit at a time. When the flour is fully incorporated, continue whisking gently until the mixture thickens and becomes a golden or light brown roux.

3. Whisk a few tablespoons of the creamy liquid from the soup pot into the roux. It will continue to thicken as you whisk. Once the roux reaches the consistency of loosely cooked Cream of Wheat, turn off the heat.

4. Whisk half the roux into the soup pot and simmer for about 3 minutes. Your goal is a bisque with a velvety texture. Continue to add roux until you reach the desired texture. Add the lobster meat to the pot and warm for 2 minutes. Finish with the lemon zest, lemon juice, sherry vinegar, and salt to taste.

5. Ladle the bisque into individual serving bowls and garnish with the tarragon. Store leftovers in an airtight container in the refrigerator for 3 to 4 days.

HOW TO SMOKE CREAM

You can make smoked cream from scratch, but if you don't have the right setup or you are running short on time, using liquid smoke is fine: According to taste, add 1 to 2 teaspoons liquid smoke to 2 cups (480 ml) heavy cream. If you are ambitious, though, here's how to smoke cream in a smoker, Big Green Egg, or covered grill, such as a Weber kettle grill. Store the prepared smoked cream in an airtight container in the refrigerator for up to 7 days.

If you are using a smoker: Soak a handful of wood chips in water. Prepare a fire and add the wood chips. Fill the water pan with ice. Add 2 cups (480 ml) cold heavy cream to a stainless-steel bowl and place it on the smoker grate. Put the lid on the smoker and allow the cream to absorb the smoke for 10 to 15 minutes. Taste the cream after 10 minutes. You are looking for a light taste of smoke. When the cream is at the right level of smokiness for you, remove it.

If you are using a Weber kettle grill or Big Green Egg: Soak a handful of wood chips in water. Make a small charcoal fire on one side of the kettle using about 10 charcoal briquettes or an equal volume of lump charcoal. Allow it to burn for 10 to 15 minutes, then add the soaked wood chips on top of the charcoal. Your goal here is to create smoke, not heat. Set the grate into the grill. Fill a medium stainless-steel bowl with ice and place it on the grate above the fire. Pour 2 cups (480 ml) cold heavy cream into another stainless-steel bowl and place it on the grate on the cooler side of the grill. Put the lid on and smoke for 10 to 15 minutes, to taste.

LOBSTER TOAST

A few years ago, when the folks at L.L.Bean—a homegrown Maine company—asked me to create a new lobster dish that started with the meat already prepped, I immediately thought of a spin on shrimp toast. Why not create a lobster toast? The tamari, sesame seeds, and sesame oil give the toast a bit of an Asian twist. Super easy, super satisfying.

SERVES 4 AS AN APPETIZER

- 8 ounces (225 g) cooked lobster meat (see How to Steam a Lobster, page 32)
- 2 tablespoons toasted sesame oil
- 1 tablespoon finely grated peeled fresh ginger
- 1 teaspoon tamari
- ½ teaspoon sugar
- 2 garlic cloves, minced or grated
- 1 egg white
- 2 scallions, thinly sliced
- 1 baguette, cut into ½-inch-thick (13 mm) rounds
- ½ cup (75 g) sesame seeds
- 1 cup (240 ml) grapeseed or canola oil
- 1 tablespoon fresh flat-leaf parsley, for garnish (optional)

1. In a food processor, combine the lobster, sesame oil, ginger, tamari, sugar, garlic, and egg white and mix to form a paste. Transfer the mixture to a medium bowl and stir in the scallions.

2. Lay the baguette rounds on a work surface and spread the lobster mixture evenly on each round.

3. Place the sesame seeds on a plate and then press each baguette slice (lobster paste side down) onto the seeds so that they stick. Set aside, seed side up, on a large plate or tray.

4. Line a baking sheet with paper towels and set it near the stove. Heat the oil in a large skillet over medium heat until it shimmers. Working in batches, fry the toasts, lobster side down, until golden, 2 to 3 minutes. Flip the toasts and fry until the bread is crispy and golden, about 2 minutes. Transfer the toasts to the lined baking sheet as you finish cooking them.

5. Sprinkle the lobster toasts with parsley, if using. Serve the toasts warm on a platter.

HOW MANY LOBSTERS DO I NEED?

When making a lobster recipe, it's helpful to have a rule of thumb for how much cooked lobster meat you will have after discarding the shells and innards. A 1½-pound (680 g) lobster will typically yield anywhere from 6 to 8 ounces (170 to 225 g) of cooked meat. In the warm months, live lobsters in the markets are known as soft-shell, or "shedders," because they have recently shed their hard winter shell in order to grow into a new one. Figure on 6 ounces (170 g) of meat per shedder. In the colder months, you are going to get hard-shell lobsters. Their meat is denser. A 1½-pound (680 g) hard-shell lobster will yield approximately 8 ounces (225 g) of meat. Don't fuss if your lobsters are 1 to 2 ounces (30 to 55 g) off for any of the recipes here, and remember, it never hurts to have *more* lobster.

B.L.T. $7.00
Gluten Free
Roll 1.50
Rolls
Lobster $25.00
Crab $20.00
Chicken Salad $5.25
$1 50

LOBSTER SALAD WITH BUCKWHEAT PLOYES

Ever since French speakers first settled in Canada and northern Maine, this buckwheat griddle cake, known as a ploye, has been a go-to. Buckwheat has a nuttier, more earthy flavor than wheat and can be planted and harvested successfully in Maine's relatively short growing season. It's said that the word *ploye* comes from the gentle *puff-puff* sound made by the little bubbles that pop open in the batter as it cooks and sets. Rather than flipping ployes, you cook them on one side only. Top these Acadian tacos with a bright-tasting variation of Maine's signature dish: lobster salad.

SERVES 4

FOR THE LOBSTER SALAD

12 ounces (340 g) cooked lobster meat (see How to Steam a Lobster, page 32), roughly chopped

1 cup (100 g) thinly sliced celery

2 tablespoons sour cream

2 tablespoons mayonnaise

2 teaspoons chopped fresh dill, plus more for garnish

1 teaspoon grated lemon zest

½ teaspoon red pepper flakes

½ teaspoon kosher salt

2 sugar snap peas, thinly sliced, for garnish (optional)

1. Make the lobster salad: In a medium bowl, combine the lobster, celery, sour cream, mayonnaise, dill, lemon zest, pepper flakes, and salt. Mix well and set aside while you make the ployes.

2. Make the ployes: In a large bowl, mix together the buckwheat flour, all-purpose flour, baking powder, and salt. Add the cold water, stir, and set aside to rest for 5 minutes. Add the boiling water and mix until the batter is smooth.

3. Heat 1 tablespoon oil in a large skillet over medium-high heat until it shimmers. Working in batches, use a 2-ounce (60 ml) ladle to pour the batter into the skillet. You will be able to fit a few ployes, each about 4 inches (10 cm) in diameter, in each batch. The batter will bubble like a pancake. After 3 or 4 minutes, the bottom edges will start to brown and the bubbles will pop. When this happens, they are done, no need to flip. You can test one ploye for doneness before you go ahead and remove them all. Set the first batch aside and cover them with a tea towel to keep them warm while you finish making the rest of the ployes, adding more oil as needed.

FOR THE PLOYES

2 cups (250 g) buckwheat flour

1 cup (125 g) all-purpose flour

1 tablespoon baking powder

1 teaspoon kosher salt

2 cups (480 ml) cold water

1 cup (240 ml) boiling water

Grapeseed or canola oil, for pan-searing

4. To serve, spoon the lobster salad on top of the freshly cooked ployes. Garnish with some dill and sliced peas, if desired, and serve immediately.

HOW TO BREAK DOWN A LOBSTER

Breaking apart a cooked lobster and getting at the meat can be a messy exercise, but it doesn't have to be. Follow these steps to break down a lobster neatly.

As soon as your cooked lobster is cool enough to handle:

1. Separate the tail by twisting it and pulling it away from the body.
2. Separate the tail fins from the rest of the tail.
3. Using your thumb, push the tail meat up and then grab the other end of the tail meat and pull it completely from its shell.
4. Using your thumb, pull on the telson (the piece of tender meat with the intestine running down it). Detach it from the rest of the tail and remove and discard the intestine.
5. Grab the claws and knuckles and twist to separate them from the lobster body.
6. Twist the claws away from the knuckles.
7. Grab the "thumb" of each claw, pull it down, and then work it out from the rest of the claw.
8. Carefully crack the claw open. You can do this by hand with the softer shell of summer lobsters. For hard-shell lobsters, a nutcracker comes in handy. Your goal is to remove the claw meat intact.
9. Using kitchen shears, cut open the knuckles and pick the meat out.

With practice, your lobster meat will look like this.

1

2

3

4

5

6

7

8

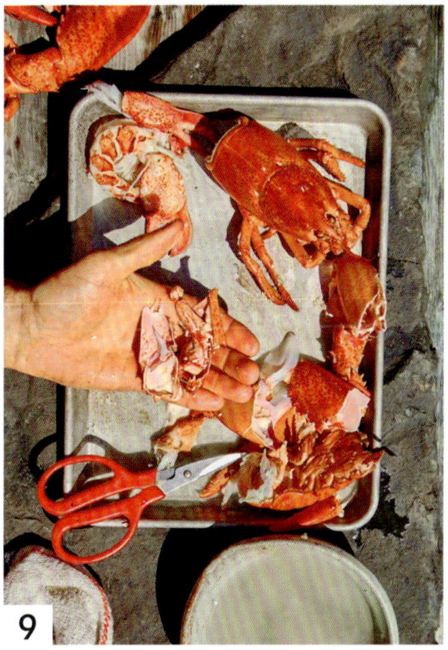
9

LOBSTAH & PASTAH

This recipe is a reflection of the places and cuisines that have deeply influenced me. Beurre blanc is a classic French combination of butter, white wine, and shallots that I learned at my father's restaurant in Vermont. Gremolata is a garlic, parsley, and lemon zest garnish that I picked up when I had a job cooking for American tourists in Italy. And lobster might as well be on the state flag of Maine.

SERVES 4

FOR THE GREMOLATA

1 tablespoon minced garlic

1 tablespoon minced fresh flat-leaf parsley

1 tablespoon minced or grated lemon zest

FOR THE LOBSTER MIXTURE

1 pound (455 g) cooked lobster meat (see How to Steam a Lobster, page 32)

¾ cup (170 g) mascarpone

Grated zest and juice of 1 lemon

¼ cup (10 g) chopped fresh flat-leaf parsley

1 teaspoon kosher salt

1 teaspoon minced garlic

FOR THE BEURRE BLANC

1 cup (240 ml) dry white wine

1 tablespoon fresh lemon juice

1 teaspoon minced shallot

¼ cup (60 ml) heavy cream

2 tablespoons (30 g) unsalted butter, cubed

Kosher salt

1 pound (455 g) penne

1. Make the gremolata: In a small bowl, combine the garlic, parsley, and lemon zest. Set aside.

2. Make the lobster mixture: Roughly chop the lobster meat, leaving the claws whole. In a medium bowl, combine the lobster, mascarpone, lemon zest, lemon juice, parsley, salt, and garlic. Set the mixture aside.

3. Make the beurre blanc: In a large skillet, combine the wine, lemon juice, and shallot. Set over medium-high heat and let the mixture reduce until 2 tablespoons of liquid remain, 2 minutes.

4. Reduce the heat to medium and add the heavy cream and butter, swirling the pan in a circular motion. Reduce the liquid until it is glossy, smooth, and lightly golden, 60 to 90 seconds. Remove from the heat, taste and adjust for salt, and set aside.

5. Bring a large pot of liberally salted water to a boil over high heat. Add the pasta to the boiling water and cook to 2 minutes shy of al dente according to the package directions.

6. Drain the pasta and add it to the skillet with the beurre blanc. Over low heat, toss the pasta in the sauce and then add the lobster mixture. Warm until the pasta is well coated and the mascarpone melts, about 2 minutes.

7. Serve the pasta in bowls. Garnish with the gremolata.

PENOBSCOT PAELLA

Although paella—a beloved dish in the Spanish-speaking world—is traditionally made with rice, you'd have to drive a thousand miles south of Maine before you came to a rice-growing region. What we do have is Black Nile barley, a heritage variety, which flourishes in Maine's climate. The smooth, slithery texture of cooked barley feels like al dente pasta. You can load up a paella with lots of seafood, as here—clams, mussels, cod, calamari, and lobster—but you certainly can make a fine paella with just a couple of these ingredients. If you find yourself in Louisiana in the spring, crawfish is a nice changeup in the mix. As with any grain or dried legume, the amount of liquid needed to bring the barley to plumpness can vary, so be prepared to add more as needed. If you can't find Maine's homegrown Black Nile barley, any good pearled barley will do.

SERVES 6

- 6 cups (1.4 L) Tidal Broth (page 304), plus water as needed
- 3 tablespoons (45 g) unsalted butter
- 1 red bell pepper, medium-diced
- 1 green bell pepper, medium-diced
- 1 medium onion, medium-diced
- 3 garlic cloves, minced
- 2 teaspoons kosher salt
- 2 tablespoons tomato paste
- ½ cup (120 ml) dry white wine
- 2 cups (400 g) pearled barley, preferably Black Nile barley (see Resources, page 318)
- 1 teaspoon saffron threads
- 2 bay leaves

1. In a 2-quart (1.92 L) saucepan, bring the broth to a boil over high heat and then reduce the heat to maintain a steady simmer.

2. Melt the butter in a 15-inch (38 cm) paella pan or a 13-inch (33 cm) skillet over medium heat until it foams. Add both bell peppers, the onion, garlic, and ½ teaspoon of the salt. Cook for 3 minutes. Add the tomato paste and stir to coat the vegetables, letting the tomato paste begin to darken without further stirring for 3 minutes.

3. Pour in the white wine and stir to deglaze the pan for about 30 seconds, or until the wine is mostly evaporated, scraping up any browned bits. Add the barley and stir as the barley lightly toasts, 3 to 4 minutes. Add the remaining 1½ teaspoons salt, the saffron, and the bay leaves. Cook for 2 minutes while stirring.

4. Reduce the heat to medium-low. Ladle 2 cups (480 ml) of hot broth into the pan, swirling the pan to distribute the barley and vegetables evenly. Cook without stirring until the liquid is absorbed, about 6 minutes. From time to time, rotate the pan to move colder spots to more direct heat. The liquid should always be briskly simmering. As the broth is absorbed, add another 2 cups (480 ml) so that the barley is barely covered.

1 pound (455 g) littleneck clams, thoroughly rinsed, scrubbed, and free of grit

1 pound (455 g) mussels, rinsed, scrubbed, and debearded

8 ounces (225 g) cod, cut into 1-inch (2.5 cm) chunks

12 ounces (340 g) calamari, tentacles and bodies separated, tubes cut into ½-inch (13 mm) rings

1 pound (455 g) cooked lobster meat (see How to Steam a Lobster, page 32), cut into 1-inch (2.5 cm) chunks

1 tablespoon chopped fresh flat-leaf parsley, for garnish

2 lemons, cut into wedges (optional)

5. Nestle the clams into the barley and cook for 5 minutes.

6. Add another 1 cup (240 ml) of the simmering broth, the mussels, and the cod and cook until the mussels open, about 8 minutes.

7. Add the final 1 cup (240 ml) broth and the calamari and cook for 3 to 5 minutes, until it is cooked through and tender, but not tough and chewy. As the barley drinks up liquid, you may need to add water to the pan to supplement the broth; always bring it to a simmer before adding to the paella. Increase the heat to medium-high for 3 minutes to help create a toasty, crunchy crust on the bottom (known in Spanish as the socarrat). Reduce the heat and nestle the lobster meat in with the other seafood and warm for 2 minutes.

8. Garnish with the parsley, scatter lemon wedges on top, if you like, and serve directly from the pan. Store any leftovers in an airtight container in the refrigerator for 1 to 2 days.

NOTES: If you have a stovetop diffuser, use it here to help spread the heat under the paella pan more evenly.

Leftovers are great the next day. I like to heat them in a hot, lightly oiled cast-iron pan, spreading the mixture out so that the barley crisps up a bit.

LOBSTER BAKE

The most picture-postcard Maine celebration is a summertime seaside lobster bake. It will take 3 to 4 hours from when you start digging a firepit to the time the feast is ready. To pass the time until the dinner bell rings, you can stroll the water's edge and let the kids splash in the waves. Ask your musical friends to bring along their guitars for entertainment. Snoozing on a blanket while your lobsters bake is also pretty chill. If a 4-hour event isn't in the cards, you can get a head start on the prep and invite your guests to show up an hour or so before the meal. Some oysters and a cold beer will get the party started. Oyster shuckers get extra credit.

SERVES 6

FOR THE LOBSTER AND CLAMS

Freshly gathered rockweed (see Note) or kelp, enough to fill a bushel basket

Six 1½-pound (680 g) lobsters

4 dozen littleneck clams or steamers, thoroughly rinsed, scrubbed, and free of grit

6 ears corn, shucked (optional)

6 russet potatoes, scrubbed (optional)

FOR THE DULSE BUTTER DIPPING SAUCE

1 pound (455 g/2 sticks) unsalted butter

½ cup (6 g) dulse flakes

Grated zest and juice of 4 limes

2 tablespoons Aleppo pepper, or to taste

1 teaspoon kosher salt

1. Dig a 2-by-3-foot (60 by 90 cm) hole in the sand, about 2 feet (60 cm) deep. Place a layer of dry rocks, the size of tennis balls or softballs, at the bottom of the hole. It's important that the rocks be very dry because hot, wet rocks can explode. Build a fire on top of the rocks with driftwood gathered on the beach or 8 to 10 logs about the same size as you would use in a home fireplace. You can also use charcoal in place of the wood; I recommend a 20-pound (9 kg) bag.

2. Light your fire and let the fire burn down to ashes. This should take 1½ to 2 hours. You'll probably need to add more logs to the fire after 1 hour to get the rocks properly hot. Rake the ashes to roughly fill in the space between the rocks. To test for the proper amount of heat, toss ½ cup (120 ml) water on the stones. The water should furiously sputter and steam.

3. To cook the shellfish, cover the ashes with wet seaweed and then place the lobsters and clams on the seaweed. If you are cooking corn and potatoes as well, add them now. Cover the food with another layer of seaweed and a piece of wet burlap. Shovel sand on top of the burlap and let everything steam-bake for 1½ hours.

4. Meanwhile, make the dulse butter dipping sauce: Melt the butter in a small skillet or saucepan over low heat on your campfire or stovetop until it foams. Remove it from the heat.

Add the dulse flakes, lime zest, lime juice, Aleppo pepper, and salt to the pan. Stir and set aside. You can also make the dulse butter in the kitchen ahead of time.

5. When you are ready to eat, using a shovel and long tongs, clear away the sand and remove the burlap and the top layer of seaweed. Rewarm the dulse butter sauce, if necessary, and serve it in individual ramekins. Transfer the lobsters and clams (plus corn and potatoes, if using) to a large platter or a tabletop covered with an old tablecloth. Each person gets their own whole lobster.

6. Before you say goodbye, make sure to fill in the firepit with sand to extinguish any remaining embers.

NOTE: The seaweed—we use a species called rockweed—should be moist and freshly gathered so that it cooks the shellfish with a briny steam. You will also need a piece of wet burlap to cover the top layer of seaweed once it is added to the firepit.

FRESH
The

CRAB

The Maine coast is famous for its peekytoe crabs, also known as rock crabs. They thrive in the cold waters of our thousands of coastal coves and are more common than blue crabs, which are abundant farther south on the Eastern seaboard. The popularity of peekytoes outside of Maine is largely due to the efforts of Ingrid Bengis, who established dock-to-dish supply lines for our crabs with some of America's top chefs. Ingrid was also a widely read author on the topic of love and sexuality. Her résumé was not a common one, but it goes to show you how Deer Isle in particular, and Maine in general, has always attracted quirky, multitalented people who have fallen under its spell.

You can use peekytoe or blue crab to make a casserole (see page 60), soup (see page 62), or dumplings (see page 65). Although lobster is undoubtedly the most popular seafood in Maine, crabmeat has its own special charms. The meat is delicate with a touch of sweetness. You'll often find lobster lovers and crab connoisseurs in friendly debates over which shellfish they prefer. Or you could be like me and love them both.

CRAB AU KEVIN CASSEROLE

My dad, Kevin, makes a version of this dish during the holidays for our big family dinner. The combination of crabmeat and melted cheese is so irresistible. In Maine, we are big on dinner get-togethers in the winter. It's one of the social events that you *can* do, no matter what the weather is like outside (provided that you have four-wheel drive). This recipe is one of my party standbys. It's especially lovely and comforting to eat while the woodstove is cranking. A crisp white wine will reawaken your palate after every flavorful mouthful. Serve with a Farm Salad (page 214) and slices of grilled country bread rubbed with garlic.

SERVES 8

- 3 tablespoons (45 g) unsalted butter
- 1 large onion, medium-diced
- 3 scallions, thinly sliced
- 1 celery rib, finely chopped
- 1 red bell pepper, medium-diced
- 2 garlic cloves, minced
- 1 jalapeño pepper, seeded and minced
- 2 teaspoons kosher salt
- 2 tablespoons dry white wine
- ¼ cup (30 g) all-purpose flour
- 2 cups (480 ml) whole milk
- 1 cup (115 g) grated Cheddar cheese
- 1 cup (100 g) grated Parmesan cheese
- 2 tablespoons chopped fresh flat-leaf parsley
- 1 teaspoon Espelette pepper, pimentón, or smoked paprika

1. Preheat the oven to 350°F (180°C).

2. Melt the butter in a Dutch oven or soup pot over medium heat until it foams. Add the onion, scallions, celery, bell pepper, garlic, jalapeño, and salt. Cook until the vegetables soften, 5 to 7 minutes.

3. Pour in the wine and deglaze the pan, scraping up any browned bits. Add the flour and stir to coat the vegetables. Cook for 5 minutes, stirring and scraping until the flour turns golden.

4. Pour in the milk and cook, stirring constantly, until the mixture thickens, about 5 minutes.

5. Remove the Dutch oven from the heat, add the Cheddar and Parmesan, and stir until melted. Add the parsley, Espelette, lemon zest, and lemon juice and mix. Gently fold in the crabmeat.

6. To assemble: Butter a casserole dish about 9 by 13 by 2 inches (23 by 33 by 5 cm). Fill the dish with the crab-cheese mixture. Even the mixture out with a rubber spatula. Bake until the casserole is bubbling and lightly browned, about 30 minutes. If you would like it more golden brown, run it under the broiler for a minute or two.

7. Let the casserole rest for at least 10 minutes before serving.

Grated zest and juice of 2 lemons

2 pounds (900 g) backfin crabmeat (see Note)

FOR ASSEMBLY AND SERVING

Softened butter, for the casserole dish

Baguette slices, grilled or toasted

2 garlic cloves, halved

8. To serve: Spoon individual helpings on serving plates along with grilled or toasted baguette rubbed with raw garlic. Store any leftovers in an airtight container in the refrigerator for 3 to 4 days.

NOTE: Backfin crabmeat is sometimes labeled as lump crabmeat. Backfin crabmeat is picked from the body of a crab and is free of shell and cartilage. Although it may contain some jumbo lump crabmeat, it is less expensive. Check for bits of shell and cartilage that the crab picker may have missed.

CRAB GAZPACHO

When the weather is hot and the air feels as sticky as maple syrup, gazpacho is a cooling way to make lunch or dinner without having to heat up the kitchen. A dollop of crab and cucumber salad in the middle of the bowl completes a filling but light summer meal. After chilling the soup, make sure to taste for seasoning, bearing in mind that cold ingredients often want a bit more salt.

SERVES 4 TO 6

FOR THE GAZPACHO

3 pounds (1.4 kg) ripe tomatoes, roughly chopped

1 cucumber, peeled, seeded, and roughly diced

1 red bell pepper, roughly chopped

1 red onion, roughly chopped

3 garlic cloves, roughly chopped

1 jalapeño pepper, seeded and roughly chopped

½ cup (120 ml) olive oil

2 tablespoons sherry vinegar

1 teaspoon kosher salt

FOR THE CRAB SALAD

2 cucumbers, peeled, seeded, and medium-diced

1 pound (455 g) backfin crabmeat (see Note, page 61)

1 small jalapeño pepper, seeded and finely diced

Grated zest and juice of 1 lime

2 tablespoons chopped fresh cilantro

1 tablespoon finely diced shallot

1 teaspoon kosher salt

FOR SERVING

Kosher salt

Olive oil, for drizzling

Chopped fresh cilantro, for garnish

1. Make the gazpacho: In a food processor or blender, combine the tomatoes, cucumber, bell pepper, onion, garlic, and jalapeño. Pulse a few times, and then, with the motor running, add the olive oil, sherry vinegar, and salt. Pour the soup into a bowl, seal with plastic wrap, and refrigerate for 1 to 2 hours to chill the soup and allow the flavors to meld.

2. Make the crab salad: Measure out ¼ cup (60 g) of the diced cucumbers and set aside for garnish. Place the remaining cucumbers in a medium bowl and add the crabmeat, jalapeño,

lime zest, lime juice, cilantro, shallot, and salt. Mix by hand to combine.

3. To serve: Remove the gazpacho from the refrigerator and season with salt to taste. Ladle the soup into individual bowls and place a hefty dollop of crab mixture in each bowl. Drizzle with olive oil and garnish with the reserved cucumber and some cilantro.

CRAB DUMPLINGS IN TIDAL BROTH

This is a Maine version of a beggar's purse—a Chinese dumpling that gets its name from the way the dumpling wrapper is bunched up like a hobo's bundle in a children's story book. From the time my girls were old enough to play around with dough, we have enjoyed making this recipe together. Little hands are just the right size for this task. Served in Tidal Broth, the dumplings are a robustly flavored starter or main course. They are also wonderful with soy sauce, minced garlic, Furikake (page 149), or ponzu.

MAKES 24 DUMPLINGS

FOR THE DUMPLING WRAPPERS (SEE NOTES)

2 cups (250 g) all-purpose flour, plus more for rolling out

1 teaspoon kosher salt

2 tablespoons olive oil

¾ cup (180 ml) boiling water

Cornstarch, for dusting

FOR THE CRABMEAT FILLING

1 ear corn, shucked

1 pound (455 g) backfin crabmeat (see Note, page 61)

½ cup (112 g) mascarpone

¼ cup (35 g) minced shallot

1 jalapeño pepper, seeded and minced

Grated zest and juice of 1 lemon

ingredients continue

1. Make the dumpling wrappers: In a medium bowl, combine the flour and salt. Add the olive oil and slowly pour in the boiling water while stirring the mixture with a silicone spatula or wooden spoon. The dough will come together quickly. You may want to use your hands as well to fully incorporate the ingredients. Be careful—the dough may be hot. Use your hands to form the dough into a ball and then turn the dough out onto a work surface lightly dusted with cornstarch. Roughly knead for 3 or 4 turns, about 1 minute. Cover the dough with a damp towel and let it rest at room temperature for 30 minutes.

2. Using a knife, divide the dough into 4 equal portions. On a floured work surface, roll one piece of dough into a log. Cut it crosswise into 6 equal pieces. Repeat with the remaining dough. Roll out each piece to a ⅛-inch (3 mm) thickness. Add more flour to the rolling surface as needed to prevent the dough from sticking. Using a biscuit cutter, cookie cutter, or sturdy glass, cut the flattened dough into rounds about 4 inches (10 cm) in diameter (see photos, page 67). Lay the rounds out on a piece of parchment paper. When you have filled up one sheet of parchment, lay another sheet on top of it and place the remaining dough rounds on that sheet. This will keep the rounds from sticking to one another. You may need three sheets of parchment to accommodate all of the rounds.

recipe continues

- 1 tablespoon finely chopped fresh chives
- 1 teaspoon Espelette pepper or red pepper flakes
- Kosher salt

FOR ASSEMBLY AND SERVING

- 1 tablespoon cornstarch
- 2 tablespoons grapeseed or canola oil
- 3 cups (720 ml) Tidal Broth (page 304)
- 3 scallions, green parts only, thinly sliced lengthwise
- 2 tablespoons finely chopped fresh chives or fresh herb of your choice

3. Make the crabmeat filling: Start by charring the corn either on a grill or on the stovetop. For a charcoal grill, prepare a fire, and when you have a bed of coals, char the corn for a few minutes, using tongs to turn the corn as each part chars, 3 to 4 minutes. For a gas grill, char the corn over high heat. On a gas stovetop, use tongs to hold the corn over the flame to char the kernels.

4. Scrape the charred kernels into a medium bowl. Add the crabmeat, mascarpone, shallot, jalapeño, lemon zest, lemon juice, chives, and Espelette. Add salt to taste. Stir with a rubber spatula or wooden spoon.

5. To assemble: In a small bowl, dissolve the cornstarch in 1 cup (240 ml) water using a small whisk or a fork. Wet your fingertip in the cornstarch solution and gently rub your fingertip along the outside edge of each dough round (see photos). This will help the dough to adhere and seal in the filling when you fold and bunch the round.

6. Line a baking sheet with parchment paper and set it nearby. Place 1 heaping tablespoon of the crabmeat filling in the middle of each dough round. Bunch up the opposing sides of the round and pinch them together (see photo). Give each bundle a gentle twist. With the dumpling upright, lightly press down to flatten the base and briefly set aside on the lined baking sheet.

7. Line a plate, tray, or cutting board with paper towels and set it near the stove, along with a spatter screen if you have one. Heat the oil in a large skillet over medium-high heat until it shimmers. Working in batches, add 4 to 6 dumplings to the skillet, base side down. After 1 to 2 minutes, the dumplings will start to sizzle and then turn lightly golden on the bottom. Carefully—to avoid spatter—add ¼ cup (60 ml) water to the skillet and cover with a lid to steam the dumplings. After 3 minutes, remove the lid and continue to cook, with the spatter screen if using, until the water has evaporated, about 1 minute. Transfer the cooked dumplings to the lined plate.

8. When ready to serve: Warm the broth in a saucepan. Divide the dumplings among wide soup bowls and ladle in about ½ cup (120 ml) of broth. Garnish with scallion greens and chives.

NOTES: If you don't want to make your own dumpling wrappers, you can use store-bought wonton or gyoza wrappers instead.

The dumplings can be assembled ahead and refrigerated for 1 day or frozen for up to 2 months. To freeze them, place them in a container in single layers, with the layers separated by parchment or wax paper. Cook directly from frozen in liberally salted boiling water, 5 to 7 minutes.

OYSTERS

The Abenaki people, who lived in Maine for thousands of years before Europeans arrived, feasted on oysters more than any other sea creature. On Deer Isle, though, the water was borderline too cold for wild oysters to flourish as they did a little farther south in Damariscotta. Then, in 2015, sustainable oyster farming came to Deer Isle, when Abby Barrows, a young marine biologist, returned home from her research in Tasmania and Antarctica. She tethered floating rafts of oysters in the top, warmer layer of sea water in a protected cove, where four daily tides provided a constantly replenished source of plankton that allowed the oysters to grow plump and flavorful. This has been a big win for the local economy as well as the environment; a single oyster can filter up to 50 gallons of water per day! I farm my own oysters now in Crockett Cove, a five-minute boat ride away in my 17-foot skiff.

I've probably served a few hundred thousand oysters over the years. To keep things interesting, I often dress oysters with tangy mignonettes (see pages 72, 76, 83) that showcase, but never dominate, these delicate gifts of the sea. You can also grill or roast the oysters to make a modern spin on oysters Rockefeller (see page 81).

GRUNDÉNS

OYSTERS WITH WILD STRAWBERRY MIGNONETTE

Wild strawberries are the first pickable fruits of the year in Maine, so they are quite special. They stand out like little red beacons on woodland paths. It takes a bit of self-control to keep from eating all of them as you go berry picking. But if you tame the urge to consume, they can become the highlight of a fruity and tangy mignonette. Farmers' market strawberries, which are much larger than their wild cousins, work well, too. In season, you can substitute blueberries or raspberries in your mignonette. Like most mignonettes, this one gets its sharp and tangy bite from shallots and vinegar.

SERVES 4 AS AN APPETIZER

12 wild strawberries or 4 roughly chopped market strawberries

¼ cup (60 ml) champagne vinegar

¼ cup (60 ml) rice vinegar

2 tablespoons mirin

1 medium shallot, finely diced

¼ teaspoon freshly cracked black pepper

2 dozen oysters

Rock salt or cracked ice, for serving

1. In a medium bowl, combine the strawberries, both vinegars, the mirin, shallot, and pepper and gently stir. Refrigerate the mixture in a covered container for at least a few hours to allow the flavor to develop before serving. (Store the mignonette in the refrigerator for up to 5 days.)

2. Shuck the oysters (see How to Shuck an Oyster, page 74) and arrange them on a bed of rock salt or cracked ice. This will anchor the oysters so they don't slip around. Spoon mignonette over each oyster and serve.

HOW TO SHUCK AN OYSTER

When it comes to oysters, there are two kinds of people: people who have cut the palm of their hand at least once when trying to shuck an oyster and people who have never tried to shuck an oyster.

I belong to Group #1, and to keep you from joining that club, here is my advice on how to use an oyster knife and a kitchen towel to safely shuck an oyster. As is the case for many skills, the more you practice, the better you'll get. You can usually buy an oyster knife wherever you get your oysters or you can order one online (see Resources, page 318).

Plan to shuck your oysters *just* before serving them, placing them on a bed of ice as each one is shucked.

Here's how to shuck:

1. Prepare a tray or platter with cracked ice to set the oysters on as you shuck them.
2. After rinsing and scrubbing the oysters, place one on a kitchen towel, flat side up, with the hinge of the oyster facing you.
3. Fold the towel over the oyster and press down on it with your nondominant hand, holding the oyster knife in your dominant hand.
4. Work the oyster knife into the hinge of the oyster. That's where the top shell and bottom shell come together. It will take a bit of probing and some pressure until you find the sweet spot and the muscle holding the shell closed relaxes. When it does, twist the knife to pop the shell open.
5. Slide the knife along the bottom rim of the shell to release the top. Discard the top.
6. Cupping the oyster in one hand, slide the knife under the meat of the oyster to loosen it from the shell. Handle with care so you don't lose any of the precious oyster liquor.
7. Lay each oyster on the bed of ice and discard the empty half shells.

Go ahead and slurp one down. You earned it.

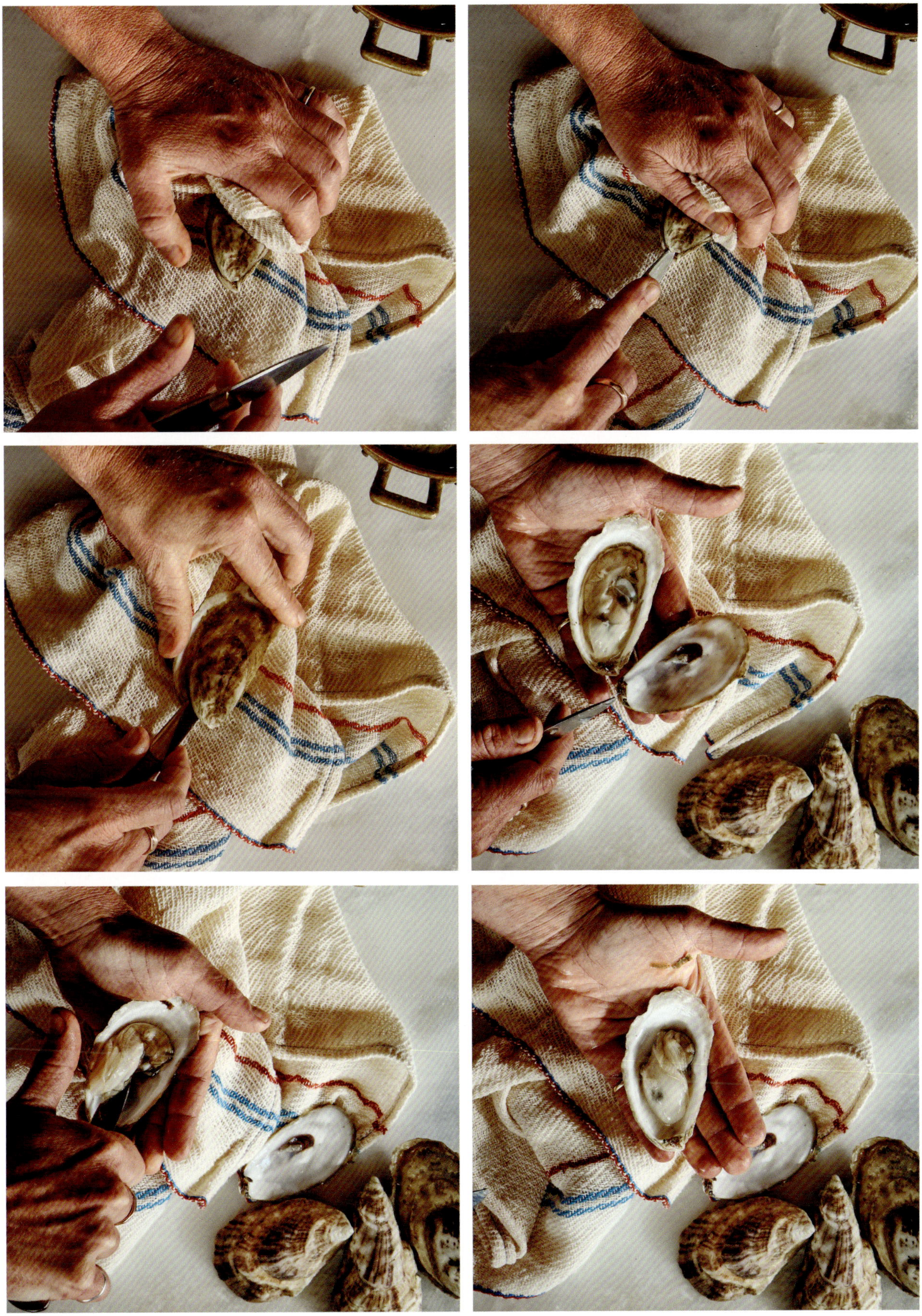

OYSTERS WITH SUGAR KELP MIGNONETTE

Sugar kelp, a kind of seaweed, grows along the Maine shoreline. We often come across it draped along the mooring lines of fishing boats. It is full of umami, which boosts the savoriness of other ingredients. On Deer Isle, we harvest whatever kelp we need, but if you don't live near a coast where sugar kelp grows, you can find kombu—which is dried sugar kelp—in many markets as well as online (see Resources, page 318).

SERVES 4 AS AN APPETIZER

- ¼ cup (20 g) fresh sugar kelp or minced rehydrated dried kombu (see Note)
- ⅓ cup (80 ml) rice vinegar
- ¼ cup (60 ml) sake
- 2 tablespoons ponzu
- 2 tablespoons mirin
- 1 tablespoon hijiki seaweed
- 2 teaspoons finely grated peeled fresh ginger
- 1 teaspoon prepared horseradish
- 2 dozen oysters
- 1 tablespoon tobiko or any fresh fish roe (optional)

1. If using fresh sugar kelp, set up a bowl of equal parts ice and water and set it near the stove. Bring a small pot of water to a boil over high heat.

2. Drop the kelp into the boiling water and blanch for 30 seconds. Remove the kelp from the pot and immediately shock it in the ice water, then drain in a colander, mince, and briefly set aside.

3. In a medium bowl, combine the kelp (or minced kombu), vinegar, sake, ponzu, mirin, hijiki, ginger, and horseradish.

4. Shuck the oysters (see How to Shuck an Oyster, page 74) and arrange them on a bed of rock salt or cracked ice. This will anchor the oysters so they don't slip around. Spoon the kelp mignonette over each oyster. If using tobiko, top each oyster with about ¼ teaspoon before serving.

NOTE: Rehydrate dried kombu by soaking it in cool water for 2 hours.

SAILOR'S WAY
STONINGTON, ME

KRISTINA - KATIE
STONINGTON, ME

GRILLED OYSTERS WITH GARDEN VEGETABLES AND DULSE

This is my play on oysters Rockefeller, an American Gilded Age recipe that is basically oysters baked in creamed spinach. Here you'll use torn kale, slivered leeks, and dulse flakes. The dulse is the difference maker: Without announcing itself very strongly, it manages to bring all the other flavors together. Think of the conductor of a symphony: She doesn't play a note, but she expertly pulls all the instruments into beautiful harmony. If making this outdoors, use a covered grill, such as a Weber kettle, Big Green Egg, or gas grill. If cooking indoors, a home oven will be fine.

SERVES 4 AS AN APPETIZER

- Kosher salt
- 12 sugar snap peas
- 2 tablespoons (30 g) unsalted butter
- 1 leek, white part only, well rinsed and thinly sliced
- 5 baby kale leaves, midribs removed, leaves cut into thin ribbons
- 2 teaspoons all-purpose flour
- ½ cup (120 ml) heavy cream
- 2 tablespoons dulse flakes
- ½ teaspoon grated lemon zest
- 1 teaspoon fresh lemon juice
- 2 dozen oysters

1. Set up a bowl of equal parts ice and water and set it near the stove. In a medium saucepan, bring 4 cups (960 ml) liberally salted water to a rolling boil over high heat. Add the snap peas to the pot and blanch for 15 seconds. Remove the snap peas from the saucepan using a slotted spoon and immediately shock them in the ice water so they stay bright green and crispy. Remove them from the ice bath and pull the strings off each snap pea. Thinly slice the peas diagonally and set aside.

2. Melt the butter in a large skillet over medium heat until it foams. Add the leek and cook for 1 minute. Add the kale and cook until the vegetables are soft, 5 to 7 minutes.

3. Sprinkle the flour over the vegetables and cook for another minute while stirring to coat the vegetables. Pour in the heavy cream and stir until it starts to thicken, 1 to 2 minutes. Add the snap peas, dulse flakes, lemon zest, and lemon juice and cook for 1 minute. Add salt to taste and set the mixture aside in a small bowl.

4. To grill the oysters: Prepare a grill to medium-high heat. For a charcoal grill, the fire is ready when you can hold your hand 4 inches (10 cm) above the grate for a full 3 seconds before it feels too hot. For a gas grill, turn it to high a few minutes before setting the oysters on the grill.

Place the oysters on the hot grill until they start to bubble, 2 to 3 minutes. Remove the oysters from the grill but leave the grill on. Using an oyster knife and holding each oyster with a kitchen towel to avoid burning your hand, shuck the oysters (cooked oysters are much easier to shuck than raw oysters). Discard the empty top shells.

To oven-bake the oysters: Preheat the oven to 375°F (190°C). Using a baking sheet, pour out salt and form the salt into 24 individual mounds; place the oysters on the salt to anchor them. Roast the oysters in the oven until they start to bubble, 3 to 5 minutes. Remove the baking sheet from the oven but leave the oven on. Using an oyster knife and holding each oyster with a kitchen towel to avoid burning your hand, shuck the oysters and discard the empty top shells.

5. Spoon the topping onto each oyster, about 1 teaspoon per oyster, and place the dressed oysters back on the grill or on the baking sheet and into the oven. Cook for 4 to 5 minutes, until the topping bubbles.

6. Carefully arrange the oysters on a platter and serve.

OYSTERS WITH APPLE AND BACON MIGNONETTE

In the fall, when sweater weather comes to Maine, the maples turn blaze orange and the blueberry barrens lie on the meadows like a faded red carpet. There is a kind of season-changing excitement to gathering by a campfire for an autumn cookout. I love starting the feast with oysters, roasted over a wood fire and topped with smoky bacon, apple juice, and sharp, tangy pickled mustard seeds. Summer is gone, but the cool crisp air of fall and the rosy cheeks on both adults and children make you feel so alive.

SERVES 4 AS AN APPETIZER

3 slices bacon, medium-diced

1 large shallot, finely diced

¼ cup (60 ml) apple juice

¼ cup (60 ml) apple cider vinegar

2 teaspoons Dijon mustard

2 teaspoons Pickled Mustard Seeds (recipe follows)

2 teaspoons ground coriander

2 tablespoons finely chopped fresh tarragon

Kosher salt

2 dozen oysters

½ green apple, peeled, cored, and finely diced

1. Line a plate with paper towels. Fry the bacon bits in a small saucepan over medium heat until they are crispy and browned, about 5 minutes. Transfer the bacon to the lined plate and leave the bacon fat in the saucepan.

2. Add the shallot to the pan and cook in the bacon grease until soft and translucent, 1 to 2 minutes. Remove the pan from the heat and set aside.

3. In a small bowl, whisk together the apple juice, vinegar, mustard, pickled mustard seeds, coriander, and bacon bits. Pour the mixture into the saucepan with the shallot. Add the chopped tarragon, stir, and set the pan aside in a warm spot.

4. To grill the oysters: Prepare a grill to medium-high heat. For a charcoal grill, the fire is ready when you can hold your hand 4 inches (10 cm) above the grate for a full 3 seconds before it feels too hot. For a gas grill, turn it to high a few minutes before setting the oysters on the grill.

Place the oysters on the hot grill until they start to bubble, 2 to 3 minutes. Remove the oysters from the grill. Using an oyster knife and holding each oyster with a kitchen towel to avoid burning your hand, shuck the oysters (this is much easier than shucking raw oysters). Discard the empty top shells.

To oven-bake the oysters: Preheat the oven to 375°F (190°C). Using a baking sheet, pour out salt and form the salt into 24 individual mounds; place the oysters on the salt to anchor them. Roast the oysters in the oven until they start to bubble, 3 to 5 minutes. Remove the baking sheet from the oven. Using an oyster knife and holding each oyster with a kitchen towel to avoid burning your hand, shuck the oysters. Discard the empty top shells.

5. To serve, spoon 1 teaspoon of the warm sauce over each oyster and top with diced apple.

Pickled Mustard Seeds

MAKES 2 CUPS (480 G)

- ½ cup (50 g) mustard seeds
- ½ cup (120 ml) lager beer
- ¼ cup (60 ml) apple cider vinegar
- 3 garlic cloves, peeled
- 2 tablespoons light brown sugar
- 3 strips of lemon zest, each ½ inch (13 mm) wide
- 1 bay leaf
- Pinch of kosher salt

Wild mustard grows all over Maine. In late summer we forage the seeds and give them a quick pickle that is sweet, tart, sharp, and savory.

In a small saucepan, combine the mustard seeds, beer, vinegar, garlic, brown sugar, lemon zest, bay leaf, and salt. Stir over medium heat until the sugar melts, 3 to 5 minutes. When the mixture comes to a boil, remove it from the heat and put a lid on the saucepan. After resting for 5 minutes, the mustard seeds are ready to serve. Store in an airtight container in the refrigerator for up to 2 weeks.

SCALLOPS

Seared, fried, barely cooked, or even raw, scallops have a sweet flavor that is buttery with a whisper of funk. When lobsters move to deeper, warmer water during the winter, some Deer Isle lobster boats turn to harvesting scallops in the shallows. The traditional way of scalloping was to drag a net along the ocean bottom, a method that damages the ecosystem. Scallops have also been hand-gathered by divers who pluck them one at a time—a more sustainable but more costly method. Then, a few years ago, Marsden Brewer, a third-generation Stonington scalloper, paid a visit to Japan, where his grandson is a professional basketball player. On that first visit, Marsden was introduced to the Japanese method of scallop farming—the young shellfish are suspended to mature in baskets tethered to the sea floor. This technique lets the scallops feed as they filter the water, just like wild scallops, without disturbing the ocean floor to harvest them. It's an ingenious and sustainable method.

Fresh scallops need only a quick sear in a hot pan, or no cooking at all, as in the ceviche with pickled blueberries (see page 92).

Shuck it

SCALLOP CEVICHE WITH PICKLED BLUEBERRIES AND SORREL

Scallops have a wonderfully smooth texture, which is just right for ceviche. Their brininess is an ideal partner for the sweet and tart taste of pickled blueberries. Ideally, prepare the pickle a day before so that it has worked its magic by the time you are ready to serve the ceviche. Maine wild blueberries are one of the glories of our forests and blueberry barrens. In this recipe, wild sorrel adds an herbal and tangy finish as well as a bit of green. On Deer Isle, we forage wild sorrel (it's a kind of sour grass), which often pops up on lawns or gardens, but store-bought sorrel works well, too.

SERVES 4 AS AN APPETIZER

2 tablespoons Pickled Blueberries (recipe follows)

1 to 2 tablespoons finely diced seeded peeled cucumber

1 tablespoon thinly sliced scallion

1 teaspoon minced seeded jalapeño pepper

¼ cup (60 ml) blueberry pickling liquid

Grated zest and juice of 1 lime

Kosher salt

1 pound (455 g) medium sea scallops (about 12), roughly chopped

2 tablespoons minced sorrel, wild or store-bought

1. In a medium bowl, combine the pickled blueberries, cucumber, scallion, and jalapeño. Add the blueberry pickling liquid, lime zest, lime juice, and salt to taste. Add the scallops to the bowl and gently toss.

2. To serve, spoon the ceviche onto individual serving plates. Garnish with sorrel.

Pickled Blueberries

MAKES 2 CUPS (ABOUT 300 G)

- 2 cups (about 290 g) blueberries, wild or cultivated
- ½ cup (120 ml) distilled white vinegar
- 2 tablespoons sugar
- ½ medium shallot, finely diced
- 1 tablespoon kosher salt

Pickled blueberries are wonderful as a mignonette with oysters or served with roast duck, savory fritters, or fried dumplings.

Place the blueberries in a heatproof medium bowl. In a medium saucepan, combine the vinegar, sugar, shallot, and salt and bring to a boil. Pour the liquid over the blueberries and set aside to cool to room temperature. Cover and refrigerate for at least 1 hour to allow the flavor to develop (they're even better if you leave them to pickle overnight). The pickled fruit will keep well in the refrigerator for about 1 week.

LINDSEY MARIE

SCALLOPS WITH WILD RAMP SAUCE

In the spring, ramps pop up in the low spots of the forest floor and we eagerly forage them in their short season. They have earthy flavor and onion-like sharpness when raw, and sweetness when cooked. This ramp sauce is nice for any kind of fritter, fish cakes, swordfish steaks, or grilled chicken.

SERVES 2
AS A MAIN COURSE
OR 4 AS AN APPETIZER

FOR THE WILD RAMP SAUCE

1¼ cups (300 ml) vegetable stock, homemade (page 302) or store-bought

Greens of 12 to 15 ramps

6 ounces (170 g) baby spinach

¼ cup (60 ml) heavy cream

2 tablespoons (30 g) unsalted butter, cut into small cubes

1 teaspoon fresh lemon juice

½ teaspoon kosher salt

FOR THE SCALLOPS

1 pound (455 g) medium sea scallops (about 12)

½ teaspoon kosher salt

¼ teaspoon freshly ground black pepper

¼ cup (30 g) Wondra flour, for dusting (see Note; optional)

Grapeseed or canola oil, for pan-searing

1. Make the wild ramp sauce: In a 2-quart (1.92 L) saucepan, bring the stock to a boil over medium heat. Add the ramp greens and spinach to the saucepan, cover, and cook for 2 minutes. You are looking to eliminate the rawness of the greens but still preserve their bright color.

2. Add the heavy cream and cook for another minute. Transfer the contents of the saucepan to a food processor or blender. Blend, starting at a slower speed so as not to spatter and then increasing the speed, until completely smooth. With the machine running, add the butter and lemon juice. Season with the salt and set aside until serving.

3. Prepare the scallops: Remove the scallops from the refrigerator just before cooking and cut a small crisscross incision about ¼ inch (6 mm) deep in each one. Pat the scallops dry and season with the salt and pepper. If you are using Wondra flour, put some flour on a cutting board or small plate and dust one side of the scallops with the Wondra.

4. Pour enough oil into a large skillet to generously film the bottom and heat over medium-high heat until it shimmers. Add the scallops (Wondra side down if you're using it) and cook for 90 seconds on the first side. They should be lightly browned. Flip the scallops and cook until lightly browned on the other side, about 20 seconds.

5. To serve, place the scallops on individual plates or a serving platter. Spoon ramp sauce over them and pass extra ramp sauce around in a small bowl.

NOTE: When cooking scallops (or skinless fish fillets), dusting one side with Wondra flour—which crisps more evenly than all-purpose—before cooking will create an appealing golden finish.

SCALLOPS WITH WARM DULSE BUTTER

Much that is written these days about eating locally and seasonally can be simply summed up in the saying, "If it grows together, it goes together." Combining scallops and dulse, which both grow in our coastal shallows, sings from the same hymn book. The dulse coaxes robust flavor from the scallops.

SERVES 4 AS AN APPETIZER

FOR THE DULSE BUTTER

8 tablespoons (115 g/1 stick) unsalted butter

2 tablespoons dulse flakes

Grated zest of 1 lime

2 teaspoons fresh lime juice

¼ teaspoon kosher salt

FOR THE SCALLOPS

1 pound (455 g) medium sea scallops (about 12)

Pinch of kosher salt

Pinch of freshly ground black pepper

1 to 2 tablespoons Wondra flour (see Note, page 97; optional)

2 tablespoons grapeseed or canola oil

1. Make the dulse butter: Melt the butter in a small skillet over low heat until it foams. Remove from the heat and add the dulse flakes, lime zest, lime juice, and salt. Stir the mixture and set it aside in a warm spot while you prepare the scallops. You want the dulse butter to remain liquid for the few minutes that it takes to cook the scallops. If the butter congeals, you can briefly rewarm it before spooning it over the cooked scallops.

2. Prepare the scallops: Remove the scallops from the refrigerator just before cooking and cut a small crisscross incision about ¼ inch (6 mm) deep in each one. Pat the scallops dry and season with the salt and pepper. If you are using Wondra flour, put some flour on a cutting board or small plate and dust one side of the scallops with the Wondra.

3. Pour the oil into a large skillet and warm over medium-high heat until it shimmers. Add the scallops (Wondra side down if you're using it) and cook for 90 seconds on the first side. They should be lightly browned. Flip the scallops and cook until lightly browned on the other side, about 20 seconds.

4. To serve, place the scallops on individual plates or a serving platter and spoon the warm dulse butter over them. Make sure that every spoonful of the butter has some of the dulse mixture, which may have settled to the bottom of the pan.

MUSSELS

Mussels thrive in cold water along a rocky shore. That pretty much describes the whole of Maine. If you were to stretch the ins and outs of our shores—all the bays and coves—in a straight line, Maine would have 3,400 miles of coastline. You can find mussels everywhere along it. Their shells are longer and more delicate than those of our other shellfish. I love the sound they make when you pour a bag of mussels into a pot; it reminds me of the soft clattering sound of the sea washing over a pebbly beach. The orange and yellow interior of a freshly opened mussel looks like the pollen-filled heart of a flower. Although they often require more cleaning than oysters, clams, and scallops, their sweet and supple flesh is always worth the effort in a chowder (see page 104), hearty broth (see page 107), and even a salad (see page 108).

MUSSEL CHOWDER

Mussels are plumpest and sweetest in winter. That's also the time when a steamy, savory, creamy chowder can restore your spirit. All along the coast of New England and up into the Maritime provinces of Canada, chowder is a hallmark of local cuisine. It always includes seafood, potatoes, and cream. I particularly like the tang and sweetness that a touch of sherry vinegar brings to chowder, but then, I like sherry vinegar in so many recipes; it's definitely my favorite vinegar. As for the fennel, it's an ideal partner for seafood and so is tarragon. While fennel is not sweet, it has a way of gently showcasing the sweetness in other ingredients. Serve with a crusty baguette.

SERVES 4

- 4 pounds (1.8 kg) mussels (4 to 5 dozen), rinsed, scrubbed, and debearded
- 2 cups (480 ml) dry white wine
- 1 medium fennel bulb, roughly chopped, stalks and fronds reserved
- 4 tablespoons (60 g/½ stick) unsalted butter
- 1 large leek, white part only, well rinsed and sliced
- 1 shallot, roughly diced
- 2 garlic cloves, sliced
- 1 large russet potato, peeled and roughly diced
- 4 cups (960 ml) heavy cream
- Leaves from 3 tarragon sprigs
- 2 bay leaves
- 1 teaspoon sherry vinegar
- Kosher salt
- Crusty baguette, for serving

1. In a nonreactive Dutch oven or soup pot, combine the mussels, white wine, and fennel stalks and bring to a boil over medium-high heat. Cover the pot and steam the mussels until they open, 5 to 7 minutes. If any mussels remain closed, cook for another minute or two, then discard any that still have not opened. Set a colander in a bowl and drain the opened mussels into the colander. Measure out 2 cups (480 ml) of the liquid and set aside for the vegetables. When the mussels are cool enough to handle, shuck them, discard the shells and the fennel stalks, and set the cooked mussels aside in a bowl.

2. Melt the butter in a separate medium pot over medium-high heat until it foams. Add the chopped fennel, leek, shallot, garlic, and potato. Cook until the fennel is soft and translucent, 8 to 10 minutes.

3. Pour in the reserved mussel steaming liquid and deglaze the pot, scraping up the flavorful caramelized bits. Add the heavy cream, tarragon, and bay leaves and bring to a boil. Reduce the heat to a simmer and cook until the potatoes are tender, about 15 minutes.

4. Discard the bay leaves and transfer the mixture to a food processor or blender. Blend, starting at a slower speed so as not to spatter and then increasing the speed, until completely smooth. Return the mixture to the pot.

5. Add the reserved mussels to the pot and rewarm over low heat for 3 minutes. Add the sherry vinegar and season with salt to taste.

6. To serve, ladle the chowder into wide soup plates. Top with the reserved fennel fronds. Serve with a crusty baguette. Leftovers will keep in an airtight container in the refrigerator for 3 to 4 days.

BEER BROTH MUSSELS

On late-summer evenings after the last customers leave Aragosta, we often make a simple and quick midnight snack by steaming mussels in Pabst Blue Ribbon beer—the preferred brew of our kitchen crew. But feel free to use your favorite brew. This is such a simple and satisfying recipe. Pickled mustard seeds add a sharp, bright note that goes well with the yeasty and bitter beer.

SERVES 4

4 pounds (1.8 kg) mussels (4 to 5 dozen), rinsed, scrubbed, and debearded

2 (12-ounce/355 ml) cans lager beer

4 garlic cloves, minced

2 tablespoons minced or grated lemon zest

1 tablespoon Pickled Mustard Seeds (page 84)

4 tablespoons (60 g/½ stick) unsalted butter

¼ teaspoon kosher salt

½ cup (25 g) chopped fresh flat-leaf parsley

Crusty bread, for serving

1. In a soup pot, combine the mussels, beer, garlic, lemon zest, and pickled mustard seeds. Using a wooden spoon, gently stir the ingredients together. Cover the pot, set over medium-high heat, and steam the mussels until they open, 5 to 7 minutes. Using a slotted spoon, move the opened mussels to a serving bowl. Give any unopened mussels another minute or two on the heat and transfer the opened ones to the serving bowl. Discard any that remain unopened.

2. Increase the heat under the pot to high and reduce the liquid for 2 minutes. Swirl in the butter and add the salt. Pour the hot beer broth through a sieve over the mussels. Serve the mussels in bowls, with parsley scattered over the top. Bring another small bowl to the table for discarding shells. Sop up the delicious broth with crusty bread.

MUSSEL SALAD ON TOAST WITH SAFFRON AIOLI

Mussels go well with saffron aioli, which is often made in Sicily for squid or octopus salads. Here the aioli anchors the mussels on toasted baguette rounds and adds a creamy texture. Saffron has a real affinity for seafood, which is no doubt why it is included in so many paella and bouillabaisse recipes.

These toasts are an ideal finger food and I often serve them at dinner parties and beach picnics when my guests start to trickle in.

SERVES 4
AS A MAIN COURSE
OR 12 AS AN APPETIZER

- 4 pounds (1.8 kg) mussels (4 to 5 dozen), rinsed, scrubbed, and debearded
- 3 cups (720 ml) dry white wine
- 1 medium fennel bulb, thinly sliced, stalks and fronds reserved
- 1 leek, white part only, well rinsed and minced
- 2 garlic cloves, minced
- ⅓ cup (35 g) brine-packed capers plus 2 tablespoons caper brine
- ½ cup (120 ml) olive oil
- 2 tablespoons fresh lemon juice
- 1 tablespoon kosher salt
- ½ cup (20 g) thinly sliced fresh basil leaves
- 1 baguette
- Saffron Aioli (page 309)

1. In a nonreactive Dutch oven or soup pot, combine the mussels, white wine, and fennel stalks and bring to a boil over medium-high heat. Cover the pot and steam the mussels until they open, 5 to 7 minutes. If any mussels remain closed, cook for another minute or two, then discard any that still have not opened. Using a slotted spoon, remove the mussels from the pot and set them aside. Discard the steaming liquid and fennel stalks.

2. When the mussels are cool enough to handle, pick them from their shells. Discard the shells and place the mussels in a medium bowl. Add the sliced fennel, leek, garlic, capers, and caper brine. Gently stir or toss the mixture to distribute the ingredients evenly. Pour in the olive oil, lemon juice, and salt. Add the basil and toss gently.

3. To serve, thinly slice the baguette. Toast or char the slices, then slather them with saffron aioli. Spoon the mussel salad on the toasts and garnish with the reserved fennel fronds. Serve on a platter or individual plates. As a main course, serve two toasts per person; as an appetizer, cut the toasts into smaller pieces.

MUSSELS SWIMMING IN FISH BROTH

I often poach or steam seafood in my fish broth, which is a marriage of Japanese dashi and French cuisine's fumet: two recipes from different parts of the world that enhance the flavors of seafood. Here, the broth brings out the subtle flavor of gently cooked mussels. Serve with a baguette and sop up every last drop. Slurping is also allowed.

SERVES 4
AS A LIGHT MAIN COURSE

- 2 tablespoons grapeseed or canola oil
- ¼ cup (60 ml) dry white wine
- 1 shallot, finely diced
- 1 tablespoon Dijon mustard
- 1 quart (960 ml) fish broth, homemade (page 303) or store-bought
- 4 pounds (1.8 kg) mussels (4 to 5 dozen), rinsed, scrubbed, and debearded
- ¼ cup (13 g) finely chopped fresh flat-leaf parsley
- 1 baguette, lightly toasted

1. Warm the oil in a nonreactive Dutch oven or soup pot over medium-high heat until it shimmers. Stir in the white wine, shallot, and mustard and cook for 1 minute. Add the fish broth and the mussels. Cover the pot and steam the mussels until they open, 5 to 7 minutes. If any mussels remain closed, cook for another minute or two, then discard any that still have not opened.

2. To serve, ladle the mussels and broth into serving bowls. Garnish with parsley and serve with a lightly toasted or grilled baguette.

CLAMS

Every day, twice a day, the tide rolls out of Penobscot Bay, leaving behind wide, muddy flats. Some of them extend for hundreds of yards of squishy, sandy mud. You might see a foolish crab or two that didn't get the memo to follow the tides to deeper water, as sandpipers and herons poke around in the mud for easy snacks. You will often see clam gatherers making their way along the flat, with a rake or a hoe, probing for clams nestled in the mud. In the summertime, clam diggers often just roll up their sleeves and trousers and reach down into the mud with bare hands. In the winter, when the seas are too rough or the air too cold for lobstering, you'll find the occasional lobster fisher coming to the flats, more warmly clothed, and filling a bucket with clams to sell or eat, or both.

The most common clams in Penobscot Bay are steamers and littlenecks. True to their name, steamers are pretty terrific steamed in seaweed at a lobster bake, the quintessential Maine summertime feast. Littlenecks can be used in fritters (see page 117) and oatcakes (see page 122) and in a luscious linguine dish (see page 126).

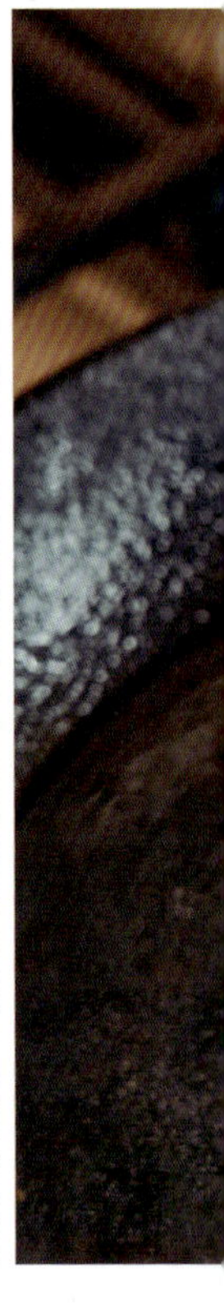

LITTLENECK FRITTERS WITH PICKLED BLUEBERRY SAUCE

It seems that everyone in Maine has their own recipe for clam fritters . . . and, of course, each swears that theirs is the only *authentic* clam fritter recipe. My recipe uses large chopped-up quahogs. You can also use smaller, more tender littlenecks (which are small quahogs) or steamers. If you can't get live clams in their shells, canned clams work fine. These fritters are light and fluffy—and even more irresistible when dipped in pickled blueberry sauce. (The sauce is delicious with fried chicken and pan-seared chicken breasts, too.)

MAKES 16 TO 24 FRITTERS

FOR THE PICKLED BLUEBERRY SAUCE

1 cup (145 g) blueberries, wild or cultivated

⅓ cup (65 g) sugar

¼ cup (60 ml) distilled white vinegar

1 garlic clove, finely grated

1 (1-inch/2.5 cm) piece fresh ginger, peeled and finely grated

Slurry: 1 tablespoon cornstarch whisked with 2 tablespoons water

1 tablespoon Thai fish sauce

1 teaspoon fresh lime juice

FOR THE FRITTERS

2 celery ribs, finely diced, tops and leaves reserved

2 pounds (910 g) littleneck clams, thoroughly rinsed, scrubbed, and free of grit

ingredients continue

1. Make the pickled blueberry sauce: In a blender, puree the blueberries. Pass the puree through a fine-mesh sieve into a bowl, pressing with a wooden spoon.

2. In a saucepan, combine the blueberry puree, sugar, vinegar, garlic, and ginger and bring to a simmer. Whisk the slurry into the sauce until it thickens. Remove the saucepan from the heat and stir in the fish sauce and lime juice. Transfer the mixture to a gravy boat, serving pitcher, or small bowl and set aside at room temperature until ready to serve. (You can make this sauce ahead of time. Refrigerate it until you are ready to prepare the fritters, then rewarm the sauce just before serving.)

3. Make the fritters: Pour 1 inch (2.5 cm) water into a soup pot and bring it to a boil over medium-high heat. Add the reserved tops and leaves of the celery to the pot. Add the clams, cover, and steam the clams until they open, 5 to 7 minutes. If any clams remain closed, cook for another minute or two, then discard any that still have not opened. Remove the clams from the pot and set aside. Discard the steaming liquid and cooked celery. After the clams have cooled, shuck them, roughly chop the meat, and set aside in a medium bowl.

4. In a separate medium bowl, combine the all-purpose flour, rice flour, salt, baking powder, baking soda, and black pepper and

½ cup (65 g) all-purpose flour
¼ cup (40 g) rice flour
1 teaspoon kosher salt
½ teaspoon baking powder
½ teaspoon baking soda
¼ teaspoon freshly ground black pepper
½ cup (120 ml) whole milk
1 large egg, beaten
½ red bell pepper, finely diced
3 garlic cloves, grated
1 jalapeño pepper, seeded and finely diced
2 quarts (1.92 L) canola oil
¼ cup (15 g) thinly sliced scallions, for garnish
A bit of fresh cilantro, for garnish (optional)

mix well. Stir in the milk and egg. Add the chopped clams, diced celery, bell pepper, garlic, and jalapeño. Stir well to incorporate everything uniformly in the batter.

5. Line a plate with paper towels and set it near the stove. Pour 2 inches (5 cm) oil into a deep heavy-bottomed pan and place it over high heat until it reaches 350°F (180°C) on a thermometer.

6. Working in batches of a few fritters at a time to avoid overcrowding, use a #16 cookie scoop or a ¼-cup (60 ml) measure to carefully drop the clam batter into the oil. Fry until golden brown, 3 to 4 minutes, turning the fritters so that they fry evenly. At first, you will notice a lot of bubbles around each fritter. This is steam evaporating as the fritter cooks. When the bubbles stop, or slow down considerably, the fritter is done. It will be nicely golden. Using a slotted spoon or spider, remove the fritters to the paper towels to drain.

7. You can serve each batch as soon as it is finished or transfer the fritters to a baking sheet, lined with paper towels and placed in a warm (175°F/80°C) oven, until you have finished frying all the fritters.

8. Serve with the pickled blueberry sauce and garnish with sliced scallions and some cilantro, if you'd like.

LITTLENECKS AND BEANS IN PARMESAN BROTH

A pot of beans with freshly steamed clams makes for a simple and hearty seafood stew. Marfax beans are a local favorite. They are fast maturing, which is what Maine's short growing season calls for. They are quite creamy and soak up the flavors of clam juice and Parmesan broth, both rich in umami. To substitute for Marfax beans, try yellow-eyed peas, though any bean that cooks up creamy, such as white navy beans or cannellini, will do just fine.

SERVES 4

FOR THE BEANS

1 cup (200 g) dried Marfax beans, rinsed and picked over for pebbles

2 tablespoons extra-virgin olive oil

4 slices bacon, roughly chopped

1 medium carrot, scrubbed and roughly chopped

1 medium onion, roughly diced

1 medium leek, well rinsed and thinly sliced

4 garlic cloves, finely diced

2 bay leaves

1 cup (240 ml) bottled clam juice (see Resources, page 318)

4 cups (960 ml) Parmesan Broth (page 306)

¼ teaspoon baking soda (optional)

ingredients continue

1. Prepare the beans: Soak the Marfax beans in water overnight. Drain.

2. Line a plate with paper towels and set it near the stove. Heat the olive oil in a Dutch oven or soup pot over medium heat until it shimmers. Add the bacon and cook until it's crispy, about 5 minutes. Use a slotted spoon to remove the bacon to the paper towels to drain, leaving the fat in the pot.

3. Add the carrot, onion, leek, garlic, and bay leaves to the pot and cook until the vegetables soften, about 5 minutes.

4. Add the clam juice and soaked beans and stir to coat. Add the broth and simmer over low heat until the beans are tender, 1 to 2 hours. Test the tenderness of the beans from time to time. Add water as needed so that the beans remain covered by about 1 inch (2.5 cm) of liquid. At this point, if the beans are a little tough, add the baking soda and cook for 5 minutes. The beans will foam up a bit, but this will subside, and the skins will soften. Once the beans are done, remove them from the heat and season with the salt. Stir in the reserved bacon bits and the torn kale. Taste and adjust the seasonings to your liking.

5. Cook the clams: Warm the butter in a separate nonreactive Dutch oven or soup pot over medium heat until it foams. Add the garlic and cook for 30 seconds. Add the clams and white

½ teaspoon kosher salt, or more to taste

2 cups (130 g) torn kale leaves (midribs removed) or greens of your choice

FOR THE CLAMS

2 tablespoons (30 g) unsalted butter

4 garlic cloves, minced

24 littleneck clams, thoroughly rinsed, scrubbed, and free of grit

1 cup (240 ml) dry white wine

FOR SERVING

2 tablespoons chopped fresh flat-leaf parsley

1 lemon, cut into wedges

Crusty bread

wine. Cover the pot and steam the clams until they open, 5 to 7 minutes. If any clams remain closed, cook for another minute or two, then discard any that still have not opened.

6. Remove the clams from the pot they have steamed in and briefly set them aside in a large mixing bowl. Strain the liquid from the steamed clams into the bean pot using a fine-mesh sieve lined with cheesecloth to remove any grit. Gently stir. Then add the reserved clams to the bean pot.

7. To serve: Ladle the clams, beans, and broth into individual serving bowls. Garnish with the parsley and lemon wedges. Serve with crusty bread alongside.

NOTE: Cooking time for beans will vary tremendously depending on how fresh they are. Really fresh beans can be soft and creamy in under 2 hours. Beans that have been stored a while will take longer.

LITTLENECKS WITH SEAWEED OATCAKES

In Wales, there is a traditional oatcake that is a mixture of oats and a seaweed called laver (the Welsh word for seaweed is *lafur*). It's the very same seaweed that the Japanese use to make nori. If you've eaten sushi rolls, the wrappers are sheets of dried nori. It wasn't until Liam Lawford, a wonderful Welshman and my second-in-command at Aragosta, pointed this out to me that I realized I'd been using laver for years only calling it nori. The Welsh recipe for laver cakes sometimes adds bacon bits and chopped clams to the batter. Here I put whole littlenecks and a dollop of miso brown butter aioli on top of the cakes. Every bite is crisp, creamy, savory, and—in a good way—clammy.

SERVES 4 AS AN APPETIZER

FOR THE SEAWEED OATCAKES

1¼ cups (195 g) steel-cut oats

6 sheets nori (each about 8 inches/20 cm square)

1 tablespoon (15 g) unsalted butter, melted

1 teaspoon fresh lemon juice

½ teaspoon kosher salt

¼ teaspoon freshly ground black pepper

2 tablespoons grapeseed or canola oil, plus more as needed

FOR THE CLAMS

4 slices bacon

2 tablespoons (30 g) unsalted butter

2 garlic cloves, pressed or minced

1. Make the oatcakes: In a spice grinder or small blender, grind the oats until they have the texture of coarse flour. Set aside ¼ cup (45 g) of the ground oats on a plate (you will use this to coat the oatcakes).

2. To rehydrate the nori sheets, break them up by hand and, in a small saucepan, simmer them in 1 cup (240 ml) water until the nori softens, about 5 minutes. Drain the nori, transfer to a food processor or blender, and process for about 30 seconds.

3. In a medium bowl, thoroughly combine the ground oats, nori, melted butter, lemon juice, salt, and pepper. Shape the mixture by hand into 8 patties, each about 2½ inches (6.5 cm) in diameter. Press both sides of the patties into the reserved ground oats and transfer the oatcakes to a cutting board or platter.

4. Heat the oil in a large skillet over medium-high heat until it shimmers. Working in batches to avoid overcrowding, cook the oatcakes until they are lightly golden brown, about 4 minutes on each side. Set them aside on a platter.

5. Prepare the clams: Line a plate with paper towels and set it near the stove. Cook the bacon in a nonreactive Dutch oven or soup pot over medium heat until it crisps. Use a slotted spoon to

24 littleneck clams, thoroughly rinsed, scrubbed, and free of grit

½ cup (120 ml) dry white wine

½ cup (120 g) Miso Brown Butter Aioli (page 308)

remove the bacon to the paper towels to drain, leaving the bacon fat in the pot. When the bacon is cool enough to handle, chop it into bits and set aside until serving.

6. Add the butter to the bacon fat in the pot and heat over medium-high heat until it melts and foams. Add the garlic and cook for 30 seconds. Add the clams and white wine. Cover the pot and steam the clams until they open, 5 to 7 minutes. If any clams remain closed, cook for another minute or two, then discard any that still have not opened.

7. Remove the clams from the pot and strain the liquid through a fine-mesh sieve lined with cheesecloth to remove any grit. When cool, pick the clams from their shells and add the clams and their liquid back to the pot. Discard the shells.

8. To serve, spread 1 tablespoon miso brown butter aioli on each oatcake and top with a few clams and a spoonful of the clam liquid. Garnish with the bacon bits.

LITTLENECKS IN SMOKY SPICY TOMATO SAUCE WITH LINGUINE

For summer vacation when I was a kid, we'd pile in the car and drive to Ogunquit, Maine, and camp out in tents. One of our favorite group projects was to scramble around for clams at low tide, feeling for them with our toes in the mud. Those summers began my love affair with Maine. Over Christmas and New Year's, when we were back home in Vermont, we didn't have much fresh seafood, so our version of the traditional Feast of the Seven Fishes on Christmas Eve included the only fresh sea creatures we could find in the market . . . clams. Every year, my dad would make linguine and clams in spicy tomato sauce. This updated version of his recipe gets some Middle Eastern smoke, spice, and tanginess from harissa and preserved lemon (see Resources, page 318). If you keep these two condiments on hand, you will never run out of ways to use them. Harissa has a spicy kick, so adjust to taste.

SERVES 4

Kosher salt

FOR THE TOMATO SAUCE

2 to 3 tablespoons olive oil
2 shallots, medium-diced
4 garlic cloves, finely diced
1 teaspoon cumin seeds
2 cups (480 ml) bottled clam juice (see Resources, page 318)
1 (28-ounce/794 g) can peeled whole tomatoes, drained and chopped
2 tablespoons diced preserved lemon (optional)
2 to 4 tablespoons harissa

1. Bring a pot of liberally salted water to a boil over high heat for the pasta.

2. Meanwhile, make the tomato sauce: Pour enough olive oil into a large nonreactive skillet or Dutch oven to film the pan generously and warm the oil over medium heat until it shimmers. Add the shallots and cook for a few minutes until they start to soften. Add the garlic and cumin seeds and cook for another minute. Pour in the clam juice and tomatoes. Bring the mixture to a simmer (you'll see small bubbles form around the edges of the pan) and cook until the sauce starts to thicken, 6 to 8 minutes.

3. Stir in the preserved lemon, if using, and harissa. Add the clams, cover the pan, and continue to simmer until the clams open, 5 to 7 minutes. If any clams remain closed, cook for another minute or two, then discard any that still have not opened. Remove the lid and turn off the heat.

3 dozen littleneck clams, thoroughly rinsed, scrubbed, and free of grit

FOR THE LINGUINE

1 pound (500 g) linguine

¼ cup (13 g) chopped fresh flat-leaf parsley, for garnish

4. Cook the pasta: When the water in the pot comes to a boil, add the linguine and cook to al dente according to the package directions.

5. Drain the cooked linguine in a colander, then transfer to a large bowl. Pour in the clams and tomato sauce. Toss well, then garnish with parsley. Set a big bowl on the table for empty clam shells and serve family style.

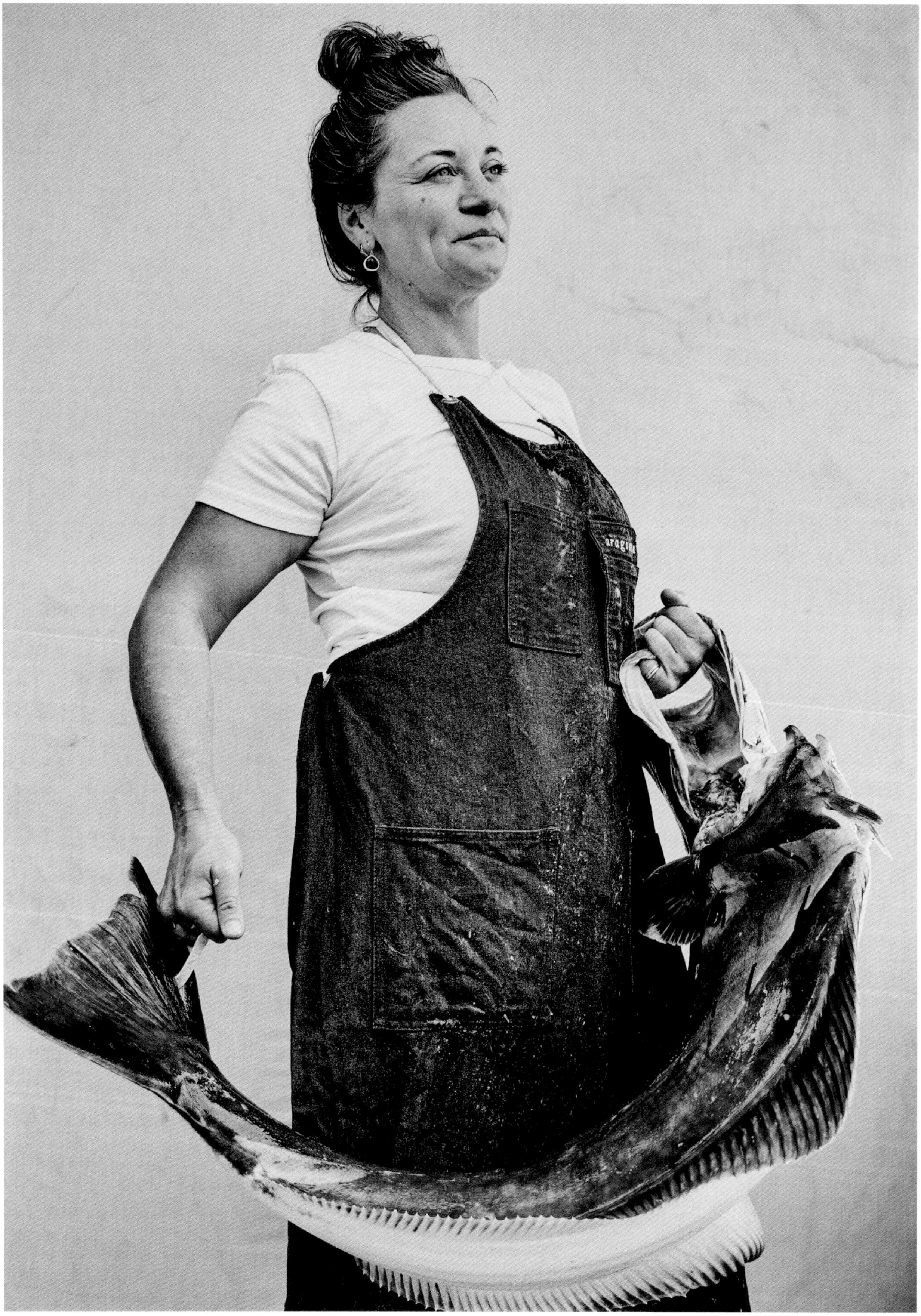

FISH

The Gulf of Maine is one of the most bountiful marine ecosystems on earth. Hemmed in on the east by the warming waters of the Gulf Stream, it is brimming with nutrients that support a rich food chain of sea creatures. Although their numbers vary from year to year, we have cod, halibut, mackerel, striped bass, bluefish, swordfish, sea-run brook trout, bluefin tuna, sharks, haddock, and hake. The fish sustain the livelihood of thousands of independent fishers, who in large part work for small family businesses, some of them stretching back hundreds of years. Our fisheries are managed for sustainability, and, for the most part, fish stocks have rebounded in healthy numbers. Every port in Maine has a fleet that fishes local waters, and the sight of a fisher in his or her oilskin bib overalls, thick woolen sweater, tight-fitting watch cap, and weathered complexion is as iconic of Maine as a cowboy on horseback is of the American West. With so much bounty at our doorstep, the question for home cooks in coastal Maine is not "Do I want seafood tonight?" Instead, it's more a case of "Which fish do I feel like eating tonight?"

HADDOCK CAKES

Haddock cakes—crisp on the outside, moist on the inside—are found everywhere in New England. In home kitchens, cafés, diners, and fancy restaurants, the appetizing aroma of fish cakes frying is pretty universal in every coastal town and village. Haddock is a mild-tasting, flaky fish that takes well to frying, which makes it the go-to for fish cakes (as well as fish and chips). Espelette pepper gives these cakes a pleasant kick, and lemon zest in the mixture brightens the flavor.

Many old-time fish cake recipes call for mashed potatoes, but I find that ricing the potatoes makes for a more uniform texture. You need to handle the cakes very lightly when coating or breading them. If you try to shape them with the same force you would use for a hamburger patty or a meatball, they won't hold together on the way to the frying pan. Rewarmed haddock cakes are nice the next day for breakfast with a fried egg on top.

MAKES 8 TO 10 CAKES

FOR THE CAKES

1 pound (455 g) russet potatoes, scrubbed

3 cups (720 ml) whole milk

2 bay leaves

2 pounds (900 g) haddock fillets, cut into 4-ounce (115 g) portions

¼ cup (13 g) chopped fresh dill

1 tablespoon chopped fresh flat-leaf parsley

1 tablespoon kosher salt

1 teaspoon Espelette pepper or red pepper flakes

2 medium shallots, finely diced

Grated zest and juice of 1 lemon

1 large egg, beaten

ingredients continue

1. Preheat the oven to 375°F (190°C).

2. Make the cakes: Bake the potatoes on a baking sheet until soft and cooked through, about 1 hour 15 minutes.

3. Set the potatoes aside until cool enough to handle, then halve them and scoop out the flesh, discarding the skins. Using a potato ricer, rice the potatoes into a large bowl.

4. In a soup pot, combine the milk and bay leaves and bring to a brisk simmer over low heat. Add the haddock and cook at a low simmer until the fish is flaky but still moist, about 5 minutes. Test a piece at the 5-minute mark. When the haddock flakes easily, remove the fish from the pot using a slotted spoon or spider and set it aside to cool. Discard the milk and the bay leaves.

5. To the large bowl with the riced potatoes, add the dill, parsley, salt, Espelette, shallots, lemon zest, lemon juice, and egg. Mix thoroughly. Break up the haddock by hand and add to the bowl. Stir gently.

6. Form the haddock cakes by scooping ⅓ cup (75 g) of the mixture for each. Roll the mixture into a ball and then flatten

FOR COATING AND COOKING

1 cup (125 g) all-purpose flour

1 teaspoon kosher salt

2 large eggs

1 tablespoon whole milk

2 cups (160 g) panko bread crumbs

¼ cup (60 ml) grapeseed or canola oil

Dill Cornichon Aioli (page 308), hot sauce, mustard, or cocktail sauce, for serving (optional)

so that it's fairly round and about 1 inch (2.5 cm) thick. Place the cakes on a plate and transfer them to the refrigerator for at least 30 minutes to firm up.

7. When ready to cook, preheat the oven to 250°F (120°C) and place a baking sheet on the middle rack.

8. To coat the haddock cakes, set up a dredging station in three shallow bowls: In the first bowl, combine the flour and salt. Beat the eggs and milk in the second bowl. Place the panko in the third bowl.

9. Lightly dredge each patty in the flour mixture, then carefully dip the patties in the egg mixture. This requires a gentle touch so that the patties hold together. Gently press the patties—top and bottom—onto the panko. To shake off any excess breading, transfer the patties from hand to hand in the same back-and-forth way you would handle a hot potato.

10. Heat the oil in a large skillet over medium-high heat until it shimmers. Working in batches to avoid overcrowding, cook the haddock cakes until they are golden brown, about 2 minutes per side. Place the crisped cakes on the baking sheet in the oven until you finish cooking all the cakes.

11. Serve the cakes with a dollop of dill cornichon aioli, if desired, or simply hot sauce, mustard, or cocktail sauce.

HADDOCK FILLETS WITH DEER ISLE SUCCOTASH

Succotash is an ancient recipe made long before Europeans first came to New England. Its name is a fun word that kids take particular delight in saying over and over before dissolving into hysterics. Native Americans made their succotash with corn and lima beans and included any other garden vegetables that were ripe and ready. I make mine with string beans instead of limas because when the other vegetables in this recipe are at their peak, so are string beans. You can serve succotash, as we do here, with a simple baked haddock for a fresh and light summer meal.

SERVES 4

FOR THE SUCCOTASH

Kosher salt

4 ounces (115 g) green beans, tips and strings removed

4 ounces (115 g) yellow wax beans, tips and strings removed

4 tablespoons (60 g) Herbed Butter (page 171) or unsalted butter

1 medium shallot, finely diced

2 garlic cloves, minced

1 small zucchini, medium-diced

1 small yellow squash, medium-diced

1 red bell pepper, medium-diced

1 jalapeño pepper, seeded and finely diced

2 teaspoons kosher salt

4 ears corn, kernels cut from cobs

8 ounces (225 g) cherry tomatoes, halved

FOR THE HADDOCK

1½ pounds (680 g) haddock fillet

½ teaspoon kosher salt

1 cup (240 ml) dry white wine

2 lemon wedges

2 tablespoons (30 g) unsalted butter

2 tablespoons chopped fresh flat-leaf parsley

FOR SERVING

Good olive oil, for drizzling

Chopped fresh flat-leaf parsley, for garnish

1 tablespoon thinly sliced fresh basil (optional)

recipe continues

1. Make the succotash: Set up a large bowl of equal parts ice and water and set it near the stove. In a soup pot, bring 4 quarts (3.84 L) of liberally salted water to a rolling boil. Add both beans to the pot and blanch until tender but still snappy, 2 to 3 minutes. Scoop the beans out of the pot and immediately shock them in the ice water so they stay brightly colored and crispy. Remove them from the ice bath and cut them into ½-inch (13 mm) pieces. Set the beans aside.

2. Heat the herbed butter in a large skillet over medium heat until it foams. Add the shallot and garlic and cook for 1 minute. Add the zucchini, yellow squash, bell pepper, jalapeño, and salt. Cook the vegetables, stirring frequently, until they soften, about 5 minutes.

3. Add the corn kernels and cook for 3 minutes, continuing to stir. Remove the skillet from the heat and add the cherry tomatoes and the beans.

4. Bake the haddock: Preheat the oven to 350°F (180°C).

5. Season the haddock with the salt and place it in a baking dish. Add the white wine, lemon wedges, butter, and parsley. Transfer to the oven.

6. Bake the haddock until it flakes. Test for flakiness after 10 minutes. Continue to test every 5 minutes until the haddock is moist and flaky. Remove the fish to a serving platter and set aside.

7. To serve: Place the succotash on a dinner plate and top with a portion of haddock. Drizzle with olive oil and garnish with parsley and, if you like, basil.

PENOBSCOT SEAFOOD STEW

Every country by the sea has some version of a stew made with local fish—big fish, little fish, shellfish, whatever creatures wander into traps, get caught up in nets, or get hooked at the end of fishing lines. In France it's bouillabaisse, in Italy they have brodetto, in Argentina it's chupin, in Belgium, waterzooi. The basic idea is the same everywhere: seafood, broth, and aromatic vegetables. Homemade fish broth adds powerful flavor to this stew, and saffron aioli is a lovely finishing touch. This is a great recipe for a dinner party.

You don't need to use all of the different types of seafood that are called for in this recipe; for a more economical version, one or two kinds will do. I use cod as the finfish, but you could use halibut, blackfish, redfish, weakfish, or red snapper. Make the dish for Christmas Eve and call it the Feast of However Many Fishes You Manage to Find.

SERVES 6 TO 8

- 3 tablespoons (45 g) unsalted butter
- 1 medium fennel bulb, thinly sliced
- 1 medium leek, halved lengthwise, well rinsed, and thinly sliced
- 3 garlic cloves, minced
- 1 pound (455 g) new potatoes, scrubbed and quartered
- 1 tablespoon tomato paste
- 2 teaspoons kosher salt
- ½ cup (120 ml) dry white wine
- 1 cup (180 g) chopped tomatoes, fresh or canned
- 2 bay leaves
- 2 teaspoons sherry vinegar

1. Melt the butter in a nonreactive Dutch oven or soup pot over medium heat until it foams. Add the fennel, leek, and garlic and cook for 2 minutes. Add the potatoes and cook until the fennel and leek are translucent, 5 to 7 minutes.

2. Add the tomato paste and 1 teaspoon of the salt, stir to coat the vegetables, and cook for 1 minute. Increase the heat to high, pour in the wine, and deglaze the pot, scraping up the caramelized bits. Let it cook until the wine is reduced by half, about 2 minutes.

3. Add the tomatoes, bay leaves, sherry vinegar, and broth and bring to a boil. Reduce the heat to medium-low and simmer for 8 minutes.

4. Add the clams to the pot, cover with a lid, and cook for 5 minutes. Add the mussels and the halibut, nestling the halibut in between the shellfish. Cook for 5 more minutes or until all the shellfish have opened. Discard any shellfish that remain unopened.

- 2 quarts (1.92 L) fish broth, homemade (page 303) or store-bought
- 1 pound (455 g) littleneck clams, thoroughly rinsed, scrubbed, and free of grit
- 1 pound (455 g) mussels, rinsed, scrubbed, and debearded
- 1 pound (455 g) halibut fillet, cut into 4 equal portions
- 1 pound (455 g) cooked lobster meat (see Notes), roughly chopped
- 2 tablespoons chopped fresh flat-leaf parsley
- 2 tablespoons fresh lemon thyme or regular thyme leaves
- 1 loaf country bread, sliced and lightly toasted (see Notes)
- 1 cup (250 g) Saffron Aioli (optional; page 309)

5. Remove the pot from the heat and nestle the cooked lobster meat in the broth. Cover the pot, season with the remaining 1 teaspoon salt, and let the lobster warm for a few minutes.

6. Ladle the seafood and broth into wide soup plates. Garnish with the parsley and thyme. Serve with slices of toasted country bread topped with saffron aioli, if desired. Store any leftovers in an airtight container in the fridge for up to 2 days.

NOTES: I use lobster knuckles and claw meat, available online from Greenhead Lobster in Stonington (see Resources, page 318). The meat is especially tender, but if you are using whole live lobsters (see How to Steam a Lobster, page 32), that's okay, too.

If you have a ridged grill pan, use that to toast the bread.

COD POACHED IN FISH BROTH

When the first Europeans discovered the fishing grounds that stretched from Labrador down through New England, the abundance of finfish, particularly cod, was truly mind-boggling. Overfishing led to a steep decline in numbers, but cod are now on the rebound. Their populations are strictly managed in the Gulf of Maine so that only a sustainable quota is allowed to be fished each year. Cod is mild tasting, with flaky white flesh and a smooth, moist texture. It takes particularly well to gentle poaching.

SERVES 4

- 1 tablespoon kosher salt
- 1½ pounds (680 g) cod, haddock, or hake fillet, divided into four 6-ounce (170 g) portions
- 2 quarts (1.92 L) fish broth, homemade (page 303) or store-bought
- 8 baby bok choy
- Country bread or baguette, for serving

1. Salt the cod liberally on both sides. Lay the pieces of cod on a platter or wide plate and refrigerate for at least 30 minutes, allowing the flesh to tighten so that it holds together well when you poach it.

2. When you are ready to poach the fish, remove it from the refrigerator.

3. In a Dutch oven or soup pot, bring the broth to a boil over high heat. Reduce the heat to a low simmer, add the baby bok choy, and simmer until tender, about 5 minutes.

4. Remove the bok choy to individual soup plates or bowls. Using a large slotted spoon, gently lower the cod fillets into the simmering broth and poach until the fish flakes easily when tested with a fork, about 5 minutes.

5. Transfer the cod to the soup bowls and, using a 4-ounce (120 ml) ladle, add 1 or 2 ladles of broth (see Note) to each bowl. Serve with country bread or baguette to sop up the broth.

NOTE: To properly poach the cod, you will use more broth than you end up serving in the finished dish, but that's alright; any leftover broth will get more depth of flavor from the cod. Store leftover broth in an airtight container in the freezer for up to 4 months.

GRILLED SWORDFISH STEAKS WITH SUMMER SALSA

Swordfish are usually found in deep water offshore, but from time to time in the summer, a lucky Stonington fisherman may catch one in our shallow local waters, sometimes as close as the falls in nearby Blue Hill. When that happens, I'm ready to fire up the grill for swordfish steaks. The meat is dense enough to hold together on the grill, yet it stays deliciously moist. A swordfish is usually caught at around the time of year that cherry tomatoes are ripe, sweet, and savory, so they are the stars of a fresh salsa.

SERVES 4

FOR THE SWORDFISH

1½ pounds (680 g) swordfish steaks, ½ inch (13 mm) thick, cut into 4 equal portions

1 teaspoon kosher salt

1 teaspoon freshly ground black pepper

FOR THE SALSA

2 cups (360 g) chopped cherry tomatoes

1 leek, white part only, well rinsed and minced

2 garlic cloves, minced

1 jalapeño pepper, seeded and minced

3 tablespoons olive oil

3 tablespoons brine-packed capers, roughly chopped, plus 2 tablespoons caper brine

Juice of 1 lime

1 teaspoon kosher salt

1. Prepare the swordfish: Season the swordfish steaks with the kosher salt and pepper and set aside on a plate in the refrigerator to chill for at least 1 hour.

2. Meanwhile, make the salsa: In a medium bowl, combine the cherry tomatoes, leek, garlic, jalapeño, olive oil, capers, caper brine, lime juice, and kosher salt. If not using immediately, refrigerate until ready to use.

3. When ready to grill: Prepare an outdoor grill to medium-high heat or, if cooking inside, preheat a ridged grill pan over medium-high heat for a few minutes. For a charcoal grill, the fire is ready when you can hold your hand 4 inches (10 cm) above the grate for a full 3 seconds before it feels too hot. For a gas grill, turn it to high a few minutes before cooking the swordfish.

4. Just before cooking the steaks, brush the grill grate or ridged grill pan with a lightly oiled paper towel. A light coating of oil is all you need. Too much oil can create flare-ups of hot oil from an open fire.

5. Remove the swordfish steaks from the refrigerator and place on the grill grate or ridged grill pan. Grill for 4 to 5 minutes on one side, then turn the fish over and grill the other side until it reaches an internal temperature of 130°F (55°C), 4 to 5 minutes. Remove the fish from the heat and let rest for 5 minutes.

FOR GRILLING AND SERVING

Grapeseed or canola oil, for the grill

1 lime, cut into wedges

2 scallions, green part only, thinly sliced

Flaky salt

6. To serve: Place the steaks on a platter or individual serving plates and top with the salsa, a squeeze of lime, the scallion greens, and flaky salt.

SEARED BLUEFIN STEAKS WITH TONNATO SAUCE

Bluefin tuna are the biggest wild creatures a Mainer can prepare for the table (unless you happen to be a moose hunter). Bluefin ride up our coast on the warm water that swirls off the Gulf Stream. A mature fish can weigh more than a thousand pounds. Not long ago, bluefin were an endangered species, but they've come back thanks to the conservation practices of commercial as well as sportfishers. I learned about tonnato sauce on my first trip to Italy. Preparing meals for American tourists, I worked in the kitchen alongside some great Italian home cooks—aren't they all?—who served this sauce to accompany thinly sliced roast veal. It wasn't much of a stretch for me to try it with quickly seared bluefin.

SERVES 4

FOR THE TONNATO SAUCE

1 (6-ounce/170 g) can tuna in oil, drained

1 large egg

Grated zest and juice of 1 lemon

1 tablespoon soy sauce

1 teaspoon Thai fish sauce

1½ cups (360 ml) grapeseed or canola oil

FOR THE TUNA

½ cup (120 ml) soy sauce

3 scallions, thinly sliced

2 tablespoons dark brown sugar

2 tablespoons toasted sesame oil

2 garlic cloves, minced

ingredients continue

1. Make the tonnato sauce: In a food processor or blender, combine the canned tuna, egg, lemon zest, lemon juice, soy sauce, and fish sauce and pulse a few times. With the machine running, drizzle the oil into the mixture until the sauce thickens to the consistency of a loose mayonnaise, about 1 minute. Transfer the sauce to a medium bowl or container and set aside in the refrigerator for up to 3 days.

2. Prepare the tuna: In a medium bowl, combine the soy sauce, half of the scallions, the brown sugar, sesame oil, garlic, ginger, lemon zest, and lemon juice. Stir until the sugar dissolves. Place the tuna steaks in a single layer in a baking dish or roasting pan and pour the marinade over the tuna. Refrigerate for 15 minutes, flip the tuna, and refrigerate for another 15 minutes.

3. While the tuna is marinating, prepare an outdoor grill to medium-high heat or, if cooking inside, preheat a ridged grill pan over medium-high heat for a few minutes. For a charcoal grill, the fire is ready when you can hold your hand 4 inches (10 cm) above the grate for a full 3 seconds before it feels too hot. For a gas grill, turn it to high a few minutes before cooking the tuna.

recipe continues

1 tablespoon minced peeled fresh ginger

Grated zest and juice of 1 lemon

1½ pounds (680 g) bluefin tuna steaks, cut into 4 equal portions

FOR GRILLING AND SERVING

Grapeseed or canola oil, for the grill

2 tablespoons furikake, homemade (recipe follows) or store-bought

4. Just before cooking the steaks, brush the grill grate or ridged grill pan with a lightly oiled paper towel. A light coating of oil is all you need. Too much oil can create flare-ups of hot oil from an open fire.

5. Remove the tuna steaks from the refrigerator and discard the marinade. Pat the tuna steaks dry with paper towels and place them on the grill grate or ridged grill pan. Grill the tuna steaks for 1 minutes on each side. The tuna should release easily from the grill grate or pan if you briskly insert a spatula under the steaks to turn them. If they don't release easily, give them another 10 to 15 seconds. Transfer the steaks to a cutting board or platter and let them rest for 5 minutes.

6. To serve: Cut the tuna steaks into slices ½ inch (13 mm) thick. Spoon the tonnato sauce onto serving plates, place the tuna steaks on the sauce, and garnish liberally with furikake and the remaining scallions.

NOTE: Leftover tonnato sauce makes for a very special TLT (tonnato, lettuce, and tomato sandwich).

Furikake

MAKES ABOUT
¾ CUP (180 G)

- 3 sheets nori (each about 8 inches/20 cm square)
- 2 tablespoons white sesame seeds
- 2 tablespoons black sesame seeds
- 1 tablespoon dulse flakes
- 1 tablespoon garlic flakes
- 2 teaspoons kosher salt
- 1 teaspoon sugar

Furikake is a crunchy, salty, sweet, umami-rich Japanese condiment. It is often served on sushi or to give a crunchy, flavorful finish to many Japanese recipes. You can make your own or buy it in the Asian section of your market or online (see Resources, page 318).

1. Preheat the oven to 300°F (150°C).

2. Place the nori on a baking sheet and toast in the oven until it is quite crisp, 3 to 5 minutes. Remove the crisped nori and crumble it into a bowl.

3. Meanwhile, toast both types of sesame seeds in a small dry skillet over medium heat, swirling gently until the seeds have a nutty fragrance, just 1 to 2 minutes. Remove the seeds from the skillet immediately and add to the nori.

4. Add the dulse flakes, garlic flakes, salt, and sugar and stir to combine. Store in an airtight container in the refrigerator for up to 1 month.

CHARRED CAESAR SALAD WITH SMOKED BLUEFISH

Bluefish hang around Maine all through the warm months. They travel in schools and go into a feeding frenzy when they encounter baitfish. While striped bass, sea-run brook trout, and the lordly Atlantic salmon are considered to be the aristocrats of the sea, bluefish have always been thought of as a more blue-collar creature. When prepared fresh from the ocean, either on the grill or in the smoker, they are pretty great, and their flesh has a surprisingly delicate flavor. Because bluefish have a nice amount of oil, they take smoke really well. They fill the bill in place of anchovies in this Caesar salad dressing served on charred hearts of romaine. If you don't have bluefish, you can substitute smoked trout, salmon, mackerel, or shad.

SERVES 4 AS AN APPETIZER OR WARM SALAD COURSE

FOR THE CROUTONS

½ baguette

¼ cup (60 ml) extra-virgin olive oil

1 teaspoon flaky salt

FOR THE DRESSING

½ cup (50 g) grated Parmesan cheese

1 ounce (30 g) smoked bluefish, homemade (recipe follows) or store-bought (see Note)

2 egg yolks

1 tablespoon finely grated lemon zest

1 tablespoon fresh lemon juice

1 teaspoon Dijon mustard

ingredients continue

1. Make the croutons: Preheat the oven to 375°F (190°C).

2. Tear the baguette into rough 1-inch (2.5 cm) pieces and toss in a bowl with the olive oil and flaky salt. Spread the pieces on a baking sheet and bake until nicely golden, 10 to 15 minutes. Set aside.

3. Make the dressing: In a food processor or blender, combine ¼ cup (60 ml) water with the grated Parmesan, 1 ounce (30 g) smoked bluefish, egg yolks, lemon zest, lemon juice, mustard, fish sauce, garlic, salt, and pepper and blend until smooth. With the machine running, drizzle in the olive oil until the mixture thickens to the consistency of a loose mayonnaise. Add 1 to 2 tablespoons water if needed to achieve the desired consistency.

4. Prepare the salad: Heat a ridged grill pan over high heat. Cut the hearts of romaine in half lengthwise. Trim the leafy ends of the lettuce if you are pressed for space on the pan. Rub the cut sides of the lettuce with the olive oil and salt to taste and char the lettuce for 1 to 2 minutes, cut sides down, until there are nice grill marks on the lettuce. (You can also char the lettuce over the grate of a hot charcoal fire or gas grill.)

recipe continues

- 1 teaspoon Thai fish sauce
- ½ teaspoon grated garlic
- ½ teaspoon kosher salt
- ½ teaspoon freshly ground black pepper
- 1 cup (240 ml) extra-virgin olive oil

FOR THE SALAD

- 4 hearts of romaine lettuce
- 2 tablespoons extra-virgin olive oil
- Kosher salt
- 5 ounces (150 g) smoked bluefish, homemade (recipe follows) or store-bought (see Note)
- 1 (2-ounce/55 g) chunk Parmesan cheese
- ¼ cup loosely packed (10 g) fennel fronds

5. Transfer the charred lettuce to a serving platter or individual plates. Spoon a generous amount of dressing over the lettuce. Top the dressed salad with the 5 ounces (150 g) smoked bluefish. Scatter the croutons on top. Shave the Parmesan using a vegetable peeler and scatter the shavings over the salad. Garnish with the fennel fronds and serve.

NOTE: Smoked bluefish may be available in your seafood market or in the smoked fish section of your supermarket. You can also order it online from Coldwater Seafood in Stonington (see Resources, page 318).

Smoked Bluefish

MAKES ABOUT 2 CUPS (500 G)

- 2 skin-on bluefish fillets, from a small (2- to 4-pound/900 g to 1.8 kg) bluefish
- ¼ cup (60 g) kosher salt

Bluefish vary in size. To me, 2- to 4-pounders (900 g to 1.8 kg), commonly known as cocktail blues, are ideal for smoking. If you are smoking bluefish for the Charred Caesar Salad, you'll need just 6 ounces (180 g), which will leave you leftover smoked fish that is great with Dill Cornichon Aioli (page 308).

1. The day before you smoke the bluefish, place the fillets in a bowl. Cover them with water by 2 inches (5 cm). Add the salt to the bowl and refrigerate overnight.

2. The next day, at least 3 hours before smoking the fish, remove the fillets from the bowl, pat them dry with paper towels, and place them on a wire rack set in a baking sheet. Transfer the baking sheet to the refrigerator. You want the fillets to dry completely so that they form a slightly tacky surface (known as a pellicle). This allows the fish to absorb smoke.

3. **If you are using a smoker:** Soak 2 cups (400 g) of hardwood chips in water. Prepare a fire and add the wood chips. Fill the water pan with ice. Place the bluefish on the grate and smoke them for 1½ to 2 hours at 225°F (110°C). When the bluefish are properly smoked, they will have a mahogany color.

If you are using a Weber kettle or Big Green Egg: Soak 2 cups (400 g) of hardwood chips in water. Make a small charcoal fire on one side of the kettle using 20 to 30 charcoal briquettes or an equal volume of lump charcoal. Allow it to burn down for 15 to 20 minutes, then add the soaked wood chips on top. Place the bluefish on the grate, cover, and smoke them for 1½ to 2 hours at 225°F (110°C). You can regulate the temperature on your grill by adjusting the air vents. An old-fashioned meat thermometer (not a digital one), stuck into the vent on top of the Weber kettle, will display the temperature inside the grill. When the bluefish are properly smoked, they will have a mahogany color.

4. When the bluefish are cool enough to handle, flake off whatever you will be using immediately and refrigerate the remainder for up to 5 days.

HALIBUT AND FIDDLEHEADS

When the curtain goes up on halibut season in the Gulf of Maine, we finally get the feeling that spring has sprung, and I am SOOO ready for it! It's also the time of year when the spring sun warms the forest floor and sprouts of fiddlehead ferns spring up, so green they look as if they were lit from within. They are a natural partner for halibut fillets, which are thick, meaty, white as snow, and nicely flaky.

SERVES 4 AS A MAIN COURSE

- 16 fiddlehead ferns
- Kosher salt
- 1½ pounds (680 g) halibut, cut into four 6-ounce (170 g) portions
- Freshly ground black pepper
- 2 tablespoons grapeseed or canola oil, plus more as needed
- 8 tablespoons (115 g/1 stick) unsalted butter
- Grated zest and juice of 1 lemon
- ⅓ cup (35 g) capers, chopped
- Pea shoots, for garnish (optional)
- ¼ cup (13 g) chopped fresh flat-leaf parsley or thinly sliced fresh basil (or both) or your favorite green herb

1. Clean the fiddleheads, rinsing them thoroughly, and trim the bottoms of the stems.

2. Set up a large bowl of equal parts ice and water and set it near the stove. In a deep saucepan, bring 6 cups (1.4 L) of liberally salted water to a rolling boil. Add the fiddleheads and blanch for 2 minutes. Scoop out the fiddleheads and immediately shock them in the ice water, then drain in a colander and set aside.

3. Pat the halibut fillets dry and season with salt and pepper. Heat the oil in a large skillet over medium-high heat until it starts to shimmer. Add 2 of the fillets, pressing down on them with a spatula for 10 to 15 seconds. You don't want to crowd them in the pan, or they will never get a nice golden finish. Cook without moving the fillets until golden brown, 2½ to 3 minutes. Flip the fillets and cook for another minute. Test the piece that you are going to eat with a fork to see if it flakes. You want the fish to be moist and flaky.

4. As soon as the first fillets are cooked, set them aside. Replenish the oil if necessary and cook the remaining fillets. When all the fillets are done, transfer them to a platter or individual plates.

5. Warm the butter in the same skillet over medium-low heat, swirling it until it foams and begins to brown. Add the lemon zest, lemon juice, capers, and fiddleheads. Simmer until the fiddleheads are cooked but still have a little snap, 2 to 3 minutes. Season to taste with salt and pepper.

6. To serve, spoon the fiddleheads and sauce over the fillets, and garnish with pea shoots (if using), parsley, and/or basil.

BUTTERFLIED MACKEREL WITH BEET RELISH

Mackerel show up in late spring, and when they do, there are millions upon millions of them. Just as soon as my "mackerel guy," Sid, tips us off that the run is on, my girls and I head down to the bait shed on Stonington Harbor and get a few herring from the lobstermen's stash. We bait our hooks with chopped-up herring and then jig for mackerel. To cook the mackerel, I butterfly them and cook them in a hot skillet. Top the rich mackerel with a crunchy beet relish and a dollop of sharp horseradish cream.

SERVES 4 AS AN APPETIZER

FOR THE BEET RELISH

2 medium beets, scrubbed

2 tablespoons grapeseed or canola oil

1 teaspoon kosher salt

1 tablespoon Pickled Mustard Seeds (page 84)

FOR THE HORSERADISH CREAM

1 cup (240 ml) crème fraîche or sour cream

2 tablespoons prepared horseradish

1 tablespoon chopped fresh dill

Grated zest and juice of 1 lemon

½ teaspoon kosher salt

FOR THE MACKEREL

4 whole Boston mackerel (about 8 ounces/225 g each), heads removed, cleaned and butterflied

1. Make the beet relish: Preheat the oven to 400°F (200°C).

2. Place each beet on a separate piece of aluminum foil. Drizzle with the oil and sprinkle with the salt. Wrap the beets in the foil and bake on a baking sheet until fork-tender, about 50 minutes. Test for doneness by inserting a skewer or cake tester into a beet. They are done when you can penetrate them easily.

3. Carefully unwrap the beets and set them aside until they are cool enough to handle, about 10 minutes. Using paper towels or a dish rag, rub the skin off the warm beets and cut them into ¼-inch (6 mm) dice. In a small bowl, combine the beets and pickled mustard seeds.

4. Make the horseradish cream: In a small bowl, combine the crème fraîche, horseradish, dill, lemon zest, lemon juice, and salt.

5. Cook the mackerel: Season the mackerel with salt and pepper to taste. In a 12-inch (30 cm) skillet, warm the oil over medium-high heat. Spread two of the mackerel open like a book (see opposite) and place them in the warm skillet, flesh side down. As the mackerel start to cook, apply pressure with a fish spatula to flatten them, about 10 seconds. Cook until the fish are golden brown on the bottom, 2 to 3 minutes. Flip the fish and cook until golden brown, another 2 minutes, again applying pressure to keep the fish flat. Remove the cooked fish from the skillet and lay them

Kosher salt and freshly ground black pepper

2 tablespoons grapeseed or canola oil

FOR SERVING

1 tablespoon fresh dill

4 lemon wedges

on a cutting board. Using sharp scissors, snip the spine just above the tail, gently lift and remove the spine and bones, and discard.

6. To serve: Spread equal portions of the horseradish cream on four serving plates. Lay the mackerel fillets on top. Spoon equal portions of the beet relish on the fillets. Garnish with dill and serve with lemon wedges for squeezing.

FLOWERS, FLOWERS EVERYWHERE

Flowers have always played an important role in my life—wildflowers, greenhouse flowers, flowers on a forest trail, flowers in my apple orchard, flowers in a bride's corsage, flowers pressed between the pages of an old gardening book.

When I was a little girl, I helped out with my dad's gardening projects around our home. He was always building stone walls and planting flowers. I probably learned to recognize different perennials before I could write my own name. We had hens and chicks, succulents growing in the crevices of our stone walls, pink peonies in the yard—as big as bouquets—and lilac bushes perfuming the air. All through my school years, I planted bulbs, tended shrubs, deadheaded old blooms, pulled endless weeds, nibbled on lily buds and nasturtium petals, and sprayed water on the roses to knock the aphids off them. When I needed some pocket change in high school, I designed and cared for a number of our neighbors' gardens.

Shortly after I moved to Maine, I earned my living as a gardener. The summer people always want lots of flowers, and I quickly found clients all over the Blue Hill Peninsula (just north of Deer Isle). I couldn't afford a car, so I bicycled from one client's garden to another. Within a few years, I earned my certification as a Maine Master Gardener, which helped me take on bigger jobs.

Each garden calls for its own plan to allow for a steady succession of flowers throughout the season. Every week is an opportunity for something new to come into bloom. In addition to the flowers that I have planted at Goose Cove—more varieties every year—we have abundant wildflowers: wild mustard as yellow as sunlight growing on our dunes, and *Rosa rugosa*, too. Violets and crocuses pop up everywhere in early spring. Daylilies reach toward the light along every roadside. In the sunny patches of the trails that wind through the evergreen forest, the tiny white blossoms of wild strawberries are a preview of morning walks with my daughters, buckets in hand, to gather the ruby-red berries. In late spring, lupines run riot in every field and meadow, standing straight and tall like a gathering of dolls dressed in white, blue, pink, yellow, and indigo.

Flowers need bees to pollinate them, so a couple of years ago I gave Mother Nature a hand and started to raise honeybees. They have returned the favor by providing me with homegrown honey. It's quite a thrill to see those bees—I think of them as my little guys—buzzing around my flowers, gathering pollen. It's a win-win proposition for the bees, the flowers, and me!

Consider scattering the flowers you grow onto your finished dishes. Think nasturtiums, lavender, bachelor's button, bee balm, calendula, marigolds, borage, and violets, to name just a few. The blossoms will add some color, texture, and herbal notes to the plate.

MEAT AND POULTRY

Although Maine is best known for its seafood, there are plenty of times when I want to cook something that doesn't have shells, fins, or gills. Just like the rest of America, Mainers appreciate juicy cheeseburgers, succulent roast chicken, and charcoal-grilled steak. Also, Maine has a bred-in-the-bone tradition of hunting, so there is often game to be cooked. It's fair to say that from the New Hampshire state line in the south all the way to the Canadian border in the far north, the grilling, smoking, and roasting of meat and poultry are well-respected talents. In all four seasons, I have a grill and smoker going down on the beach at Goose Cove; wood-fired cookouts are a high point of all four seasons, from a Tomahawk Steak with Chanterelles (page 169) in the fall to Duck Breasts with Peach Sauce (page 173) in the summer.

TOMAHAWK STEAK WITH CHANTERELLES

A tomahawk steak makes a serious carnivore statement: a massive, double-cut rib eye with the long rib bone left intact and trimmed so that the steak and its bone look like a king-size tomahawk. On a sunny summer day, a skillet of chanterelle mushrooms—foraged, cleaned, and cooked in herbed butter—is a delicious accompaniment to a tomahawk, or any steak, for that matter. One key piece of advice: Don't be in a hurry. The thicker the steak, the slower it should cook to have a flavorful char on the outside and a juicy pink color inside.

SERVES 4

FOR THE STEAK

- 1 tomahawk steak (about 3 pounds/1.3 kg), 3 inches (7.5 cm) thick
- 2 teaspoons kosher salt
- 1 teaspoon freshly ground black pepper
- Grapeseed or canola oil, for the grill
- 2 tablespoons cold Herbed Butter (recipe follows)

FOR THE CHANTERELLES

- 4 tablespoons (60 g) Herbed Butter (recipe follows)
- 2 pounds (900 g) chanterelles, cleaned and bottoms trimmed
- Kosher salt and freshly ground black pepper
- 1 tablespoon chopped fresh flat-leaf parsley

1. Prepare the steak: Season the steak on both sides with the salt and pepper and refrigerate for at least 2 hours (see Notes). Remove the steak from the refrigerator about 30 minutes before cooking to come to room temperature. Pat dry with paper towels and place on a platter.

2. If you are using a charcoal grill, make a charcoal fire and let it burn until the coals are covered with ash. You are looking for a medium-low heat. The fire is ready when you can hold your hand 4 inches (10 cm) above the grate for a full 3 seconds before it feels too hot.

3. If you are using a gas grill, turn it to medium for 5 minutes.

4. Just before cooking the steak, brush the grill grates with a lightly oiled paper towel. A light coating of oil is all you need. Too much oil can create flare-ups of hot oil from an open fire.

5. Place the steak on the grill. Cook for 10 minutes on one side and then, using tongs, stand the steak upright on edge for 4 minutes. You may need to prop the steak against the side of the grill or use a cast-iron skillet to keep the steak upright as you sear the sides. Finally, cook the remaining flat side of the steak until it reaches an internal temperature of 115°F (46°C), 8 to 10 minutes.

recipe continues

6. Remove the steak to a platter or cutting board and top the steak with the herbed butter. Let the steak rest for 10 minutes.

7. Cook the chanterelles: Melt the herbed butter in a cast-iron skillet over medium-high heat until it foams. Add the chanterelles and cook, stirring the mushrooms and browning them, 7 to 9 minutes. Season with salt and pepper to taste and add the parsley. Remove from the heat.

8. To serve, cut the steak away from the bone and carve it into slices ½ inch (13 mm) thick. Lay them out on a platter or cutting board and spoon the chanterelles over the slices.

NOTES: I make this special-occasion dish with an herbed butter, using herbs from my garden. If you don't have it on hand or don't feel like making it, regular unsalted butter seasoned with salt, pepper, and fresh parsley will do the trick.

Salting the steak well in advance allows the salt to penetrate the meat and keeps the meat juicy while grilling.

Herbed Butter

MAKES ABOUT 9 OUNCES (255 G)

- 8 ounces (225 g/2 sticks) unsalted butter, at room temperature
- ¼ cup (13 g) fresh flat-leaf parsley leaves
- ¼ cup (13 g) fresh dill
- ¼ cup (13 g) fresh tarragon leaves
- 2 garlic cloves, roughly chopped
- 1 teaspoon kosher salt, plus more to taste
- Grated zest and juice of 1 lemon

Compound butters are cold butters that are mixed with herbs and spices, mushrooms, or even truffles. In this version, the butter absorbs fresh herbal notes, the bracing sharpness of garlic, and the tanginess of lemon. I often use this flavorful butter on steak, grilled chicken, string beans, asparagus, baked potatoes, and corn on the cob.

1. In a food processor or blender, combine the butter, parsley, dill, and tarragon and blend for 15 seconds or until the butter starts to turn green. Add the garlic and blend for another 15 seconds. Scrape down the sides of the bowl. With the machine running, add the salt, lemon zest, and lemon juice and blend for 15 to 20 seconds. Taste for seasoning and add more salt if needed.

2. Transfer to an airtight container or, using parchment, roll it into a log, wrap in the parchment, and wrap again with plastic wrap. Store in the refrigerator for up to 1 week or in the freezer for up to 3 months.

DUCK BREASTS WITH PEACH SAUCE

When I was a young girl, my dad was sous-chef in one of Vermont's first fine-dining restaurants. It was a real treat when he would make some of his restaurant recipes at home. Duck à l'orange was a big hit with me and now this dish is my daughter Annabel's favorite. We have wonderful peaches in Maine; they are spectacular in this sauce and when grilled alongside pan-seared duck breasts. The trick with duck breasts is to start them in a cold pan and cook them slowly over relatively low heat so that fat weeps out as the breast cooks at a steady sizzle. Your goal is a crisp skin, little fat, and rosy-pink meat. A scattering of wild blueberries finishes each bite with a fruity pop.

SERVES 4

- 2 duck breasts (8 to 10 ounces/240 to 280 g each)
- 1 teaspoon kosher salt

FOR THE PEACH SAUCE

- 2 cups (480 ml) chicken stock, homemade (page 305) or store-bought
- 5 peaches, 3 of them pitted and diced, 2 of them halved and pitted
- 2 tablespoons fresh thyme leaves
- 1 tablespoon maple syrup
- 2 tablespoons (30 g) unsalted butter or Herbed Butter (page 171), at room temperature

ingredients continue

1. Using a sharp knife, score the skin of the duck breasts in a crisscross pattern, taking care to cut through the layer of fat but not slicing into the flesh. Salt the breasts and refrigerate for at least 1 hour.

2. Meanwhile, make the peach sauce: In a saucepan, combine the chicken stock, diced peaches, and thyme and cook over medium-low heat until the liquid is syrupy, about 10 minutes. Remove the saucepan from the heat and transfer the contents to a food processor or blender. Add the maple syrup and blend at a slower speed for 20 seconds, then add the butter and blend again at medium speed until the mixture is uniformly combined.

3. When ready to cook, remove the duck breasts from the refrigerator, pat dry with paper towels, and let them come to room temperature for at least 15 minutes.

4. Place the duck breasts skin side down in a large cold cast-iron skillet and set the heat to medium-low. Fat will slowly start to render out of the duck. From time to time, spoon the fat out of the pan so that the duck continues to sizzle rather than aggressively fry. (Save the fat. It's good as gold for other recipes, such as roasted potatoes.)

recipe continues

FOR SERVING

½ cup (75 g) blueberries

2 tablespoons fresh thyme leaves

5. After 7 minutes, place the 4 peach halves, cut sides down, in the pan and cook until the duck reaches an internal temperature of 125°F (52°C), another 5 to 7 minutes. Flip the duck breasts and cook for 30 seconds to color the flesh. Transfer the duck breasts to a plate or cutting board and let rest for 5 minutes. Carve into slices ½ inch (13 mm) thick.

6. To serve: Place 4 slices of duck on each plate. Set 1 peach half alongside, browned side up, and pour the peach sauce over the sliced duck. Garnish with the blueberries and thyme leaves.

ROAST CHICKEN WITH ANADAMA STUFFING

There is nothing homier or more satisfying than a roast chicken, fresh out of the oven, its skin a golden brown and its aroma inviting you to the table. For me, it's always a joy to present a roast bird at a small dinner party or family dinner. This moist, savory, ever so slightly sweet stuffing is made with Maine's traditional Anadama bread. It never fails to be eaten down to the last mouthful.

Roasting a chicken is not overly demanding in terms of technique—all that is required of the chef is that she pay attention to time and temperature. Be sure to take an internal temperature once or twice while the chicken is in the oven so that it comes out with tender, juicy breast meat. I like to cook chicken until a thermometer inserted into the thickest part of the thigh reads 155°F (68°C). Give the bird 10 to 15 minutes to rest before carving so the juices settle back into the meat.

SERVES 6

1 (3- to 3½-pound/1.3 to 1.6 kg) whole chicken, patted dry

FOR THE ANADAMA STUFFING

1 loaf Anadama bread, homemade (page 179) or store-bought

4 tablespoons (60 g/½ stick) unsalted butter

½ cup (45 g) roughly chopped leek, well rinsed

½ cup (55 g) roughly chopped onion

1 apple, peeled, cored, and medium-diced

1 tablespoon fresh rosemary leaves

ingredients continue

1. Thirty minutes before cooking, remove the chicken from the refrigerator, pat it dry, and set it aside.

2. Preheat the oven to 425°F (220°C).

3. Make the stuffing: Tear the bread into 2-inch (5 cm) pieces, place them on a baking sheet, and toast in the oven until they are quite dry, about 10 minutes. Remove the toasted bread to a food processor, pulse into coarse crumbs, and set aside. Leave the oven on.

4. Melt the butter in a large nonreactive Dutch oven over medium heat until it foams. Add the leek and onion and cook until the onions are translucent, about 5 minutes. Transfer the vegetables to a large bowl. Add the toasted bread crumbs and the apple, rosemary, sage, and thyme and mix. Add the apple cider and vinegar. Mix again and stir in the salt and pepper.

5. Roast the chicken: Stuff the chicken with the Anadama mixture. Truss the chicken (see photo, page 177). Lightly oil the top of the chicken and season it generously with salt and pepper.

recipe continues

- 1 tablespoon chopped fresh sage
- 1 tablespoon fresh thyme leaves
- ¼ cup (60 ml) apple cider
- 1 teaspoon apple cider vinegar
- 1 teaspoon kosher salt
- ½ teaspoon freshly ground black pepper

FOR THE CHICKEN AND GRAVY

- 2 tablespoons olive oil
- Kosher salt and freshly ground black pepper
- 1 large onion, sliced
- 2 cups (480 ml) chicken stock, homemade (page 305) or store-bought
- 1 tablespoon (15 g) unsalted butter, cubed

Place the onion slices on the bottom of the Dutch oven. Place the chicken on top of the onion slices.

6. Place the Dutch oven on a rack in the bottom third of the oven. After 15 minutes, reduce the heat to 350°F (180°C) and cook until the juices run clear and a thermometer inserted into the thickest part of the thigh reads 155°F (68°C), 20 minutes per pound (70 to 80 minutes total).

7. Remove the pot from the oven and transfer the chicken to a cutting board to rest while you make the gravy, 10 to 15 minutes.

8. Make the gravy: Place the Dutch oven back on the stovetop over high heat, add the chicken stock, and deglaze the pot, making sure to scrape up all the tasty browned bits. Cook until the liquid is reduced by half. Strain into a small saucepan, pressing on the onions to get every drop of flavor. Whisk the butter into the gravy. Add salt and pepper to taste.

9. Remove the stuffing from the chicken and transfer to a serving bowl. Carve the breast meat into slices ½ inch (13 mm) thick, separate the thighs from the legs, and serve the chicken on a platter or cutting board. Pass the gravy in a gravy boat, small pitcher, or bowl. Store leftovers in an airtight container in the refrigerator for up to 3 days.

ANADAMA BREAD

Open almost any traditional New England cookbook and you are guaranteed to find a recipe for Anadama bread. Dense and hardy, Anadama gets its rustic flavor and texture from a dough enriched with a porridge of cornmeal and molasses. The most commonly told story about its origin is that back in colonial times, a cranky fisherman had grown weary of his wife's cornmeal and molasses porridge, so he added some flour and yeast and baked himself a bread (while uttering some combination of the words *Anna*—his wife's name—and *damn*). I don't buy that, but it is one of those stories that is too good to fact-check.

MAKES 2 LOAVES

- ⅔ cup (80 g) cornmeal
- ½ cup (120 ml) molasses
- 4 tablespoons (60 g/½ stick) unsalted butter
- 1 (¼-ounce/7 g) envelope active dry yeast (2¼ teaspoons)
- ½ cup (120 ml) lukewarm water
- ⅓ cup (35 g) powdered milk
- 3 cups (375 g) all-purpose flour, plus more for dusting
- 1 cup (125 g) whole wheat flour
- 1¼ teaspoons kosher salt
- 1 tablespoon canola or grapeseed oil

FOR ASSEMBLY

- Softened butter or cooking spray, for the pans
- Egg wash: 1 large egg beaten with 1 tablespoon water
- 1 tablespoon caraway seeds
- 1 tablespoon flaky salt

1. In a deep medium saucepan, combine 1 cup (240 ml) water, the cornmeal, molasses, and butter. Cook over medium heat, whisking often to break up any lumps, until the porridge is as thick as breakfast grits or Cream of Wheat cereal, 5 to 7 minutes. Remove the porridge from the heat and set it aside to cool for 30 minutes. It should be lukewarm but not hot when you make the dough (too much heat will kill the yeast).

2. In a medium bowl, dissolve the yeast in the lukewarm water and stir. Add the cooled porridge and mix to combine. Stir in the milk powder and 1 cup (125 g) of the all-purpose flour. Mix well and set aside at room temperature for 30 minutes.

3. In a stand mixer fitted with the dough hook, combine the remaining 2 cups (250 g) all-purpose flour, the whole wheat flour, kosher salt, and the porridge mixture. Mix until the dough comes together and pulls away from the sides of the bowl, 6 to 8 minutes.

4. Transfer the dough to a bowl oiled with 1 tablespoon of oil, cover with a cloth, and set aside in a warm place to rise until doubled in bulk, 1 to 1½ hours.

5. To assemble: Turn the dough out onto a floured work surface. Gently deflate the dough, punching it down. Divide the dough in half and shape each half into an 8-inch (20 cm) log.

recipe continues

6. Butter or use cooking spray to prepare two 8½-by-4½-inch (22 by 12 cm) loaf pans. Place a log in each pan and cover with a damp towel. Set the pans aside in a warm place to rise until the centers of the loaves have crested at least 1 inch (2.5 cm) above the lip of the loaf pans, about 1½ hours.

7. Position a rack in the bottom third of the oven and preheat the oven to 425°F (220°C).

8. Brush the egg wash on top of the loaves, then sprinkle with the caraway seeds and flaky salt. Transfer the pans to the oven and bake until the crusts have a deep brown color, 35 to 40 minutes.

9. Let the breads cool in the pans for 5 minutes, then turn the loaves out onto a wire rack to cool completely. The breads will keep, tightly wrapped, at room temperature for up to 3 days.

VARIATION:

ANADAMA BUNS

1. Follow the bread recipe through the first rise of the dough. Divide the dough in two and form two 8-inch (20 cm) logs as directed, then cut each log into 6 equal portions for a total of 12 buns. Shape each portion of dough into a rough ball (see opposite). Applying a bit more pressure, continue to roll the ball. The added pressure will tighten the surface of the dough ball and create a smooth skin for the bun. Once you have a round smooth ball, lightly press on top of the ball to flatten the bottom of each bun.

2. Transfer the buns to a parchment-lined baking sheet, cover with plastic wrap, and allow to rise until they have doubled in size and are puffy and supple, about 45 minutes.

3. Preheat the oven to 425°F (220°C).

4. Brush the buns with the egg wash and sprinkle with the caraway seeds and flaky salt. Bake until the buns have a deep brown color, 15 to 18 minutes.

5. Let the buns cool on the pan for a few minutes, then transfer to a wire rack to cool completely.

CRISPY SKIN CHICKEN THIGHS

Every parent has a few favorite recipes that are easy to make and always liked by the family in their rotation. These chicken thighs are a favorite in my house. Start them in a cold pan. Don't worry about them sticking to the pan; the fat will render out of the skin, allowing the thighs to release when they are beautifully crisp. You may need to slip a metal spatula under the thighs when it's time to flip them, but have faith—they will be crispy and golden. A schmear of Greek yogurt with mint and cucumber serves as a creamy and crunchy accompaniment. Garnish with dill and diced cucumber, as well as red onions and chili crisp if you like.

SERVES 4

FOR THE CHICKEN

- 4 bone-in, skin-on chicken thighs
- 1 teaspoon kosher salt
- 1 teaspoon freshly ground black pepper
- 2 cups (480 ml) chicken stock, homemade (page 305) or store-bought

FOR THE YOGURT SAUCE

- 1 cucumber, peeled and seeded, or 1 seedless cucumber, peeled
- 1 cup (240 ml) plain Greek yogurt
- 1 tablespoon minced fresh mint
- ½ teaspoon kosher salt

ingredients continue

1. Position a rack in the bottom third of the oven and preheat the oven to 350°F (180°C).

2. Pat the chicken thighs dry with a paper towel and season both sides with the salt and pepper. Place them in a large unheated cast-iron skillet, skin side down. Set over medium heat and do not move the thighs. After 5 minutes, weigh the chicken down with another skillet or a weight like the kind used for smash burgers. The thighs will be golden brown after 12 to 15 minutes.

3. Meanwhile, warm the chicken stock in a small saucepan.

4. When the thighs are golden brown on the first side, flip them with a metal spatula, using a firm decisive stroke to release them from the pan. Then pour enough of the warm stock into the skillet to come two-thirds of the way up the sides of the pieces of chicken (as you would for braising).

5. Transfer the skillet to the oven and roast for 25 minutes.

6. Meanwhile, make the yogurt sauce: Use a box grater to roughly grate half of the cucumber over a clean kitchen towel. Dice the other half and set aside for garnish. Gather up the towel and twist to wring out the moisture from the grated cucumber, then transfer to a cutting board and chop the cucumber even more finely. In a small bowl, combine the grated cucumber, yogurt, mint, and salt and stir to combine.

recipe continues

FOR SERVING

1 tablespoon fresh dill

Pickled Red Onions (page 316; optional)

Chili crisp, homemade (recipe follows) or store-bought (optional)

7. Remove the skillet from the oven and transfer the chicken thighs to a plate or cutting board. (Save the delicious braising liquid; see Note.)

8. To serve: Smear 1 or 2 tablespoons of the yogurt mixture onto each dinner plate and place a chicken thigh on the yogurt. Garnish with the dill and reserved diced cucumber. If desired, serve with pickled onions and chili crisp, too.

NOTE: Save the braising liquid from this recipe and use it for stocks, risotto, or beans. It also will supercharge the gravy for the Roast Chicken with Anadama Stuffing (page 175) if used in place of chicken stock.

Chili Crisp

MAKES 2 CUPS (480 ML)

4 dried chiles de árbol

1 or 2 ancho chiles, to taste

1 dried Thai chile

2 cinnamon sticks

1 tablespoon whole black peppercorns

2 star anise pods

2 teaspoons cumin seeds

Seeds of 2 cardamom pods

⅔ cup (85 g) raw pumpkin seeds

1¼ cups (300 ml) grapeseed or canola oil

2 medium shallots, thinly sliced

Chinese cooks have used some version of chili crisp—a mixture of chiles, shallots, garlic, nuts, and seeds—for a long time. It wasn't until the owner of a small noodle shop started selling it under the name Lao Gan Ma (which means "old godmother") that it began to be more widely used. Since it first appeared on the global food scene in the 1990s, chefs and home cooks have developed their own custom mixes. My chili crisp has just enough chiles to wake up your palate and a blend of pungent, aromatic spices and Maine maple syrup that make it an all-purpose condiment that goes with pretty much everything: fried clams, scrambled eggs, steak, seared scallops, crab cakes, duck breast, or even a last-minute, no-recipe pantry pasta.

1. Slice the stems off all of the chiles and discard. Split the chiles lengthwise and push the seeds from the flesh with your thumb and discard the seeds. It's okay if the chiles break apart.

6 to 8 garlic cloves, thinly sliced

1 (1-inch/2.5 cm) piece fresh ginger, thinly sliced

1½ tablespoons maple syrup

1 teaspoon kosher salt

2. In a blender, combine the chiles, cinnamon sticks, peppercorns, star anise, cumin, and cardamom and grind the ingredients to a coarse powder. Set the mixture aside in a bowl.

3. Toast the pumpkin seeds in a small dry skillet over medium heat, swirling regularly to keep them from burning. As soon as they smell toasty, 1 to 2 minutes, remove them from the heat. Let the pumpkin seeds cool for a few minutes and then roughly chop. Add them to the bowl with the ground chiles and spices.

4. Line a plate with paper towels and set it near the stove. Heat the oil in a deep medium saucepan to 325°F (163°C) on a deep-fry thermometer.

5. Carefully add the shallots to the oil to avoid spattering. Fry the shallots, stirring gently, until they are a deep golden brown, 3 to 5 minutes. Remove the shallots with a slotted spoon and drain them on the paper towels, then add them to the bowl.

6. In the same oil, fry the garlic and ginger together until the garlic starts to turn golden, about 1 minute. With a slotted spoon, transfer the garlic and ginger to the blender. Add the maple syrup and salt and, with the blender running on low, drizzle in ¾ cup (180 ml) of the hot oil. (Save the remaining oil to add flavor when cooking vegetables.) Blend for 30 seconds.

7. Pour the mixture out of the blender into the bowl with the other ingredients. Stir a few times. Allow it to cool before serving. Store the chili crisp in an airtight container in the refrigerator for up to 2 months.

NOTES: Depending on your spiciness tolerance, feel free to use fewer chiles.

After handling the chiles it's a good idea to wash your hands. If you have sensitive skin you might want to wear latex gloves when you seed the chiles.

STUFFED DOUBLE-CUT PORK CHOPS

To serve tender and juicy pork chops, you need to start with great meat. Supermarket pork can often be bland and dry. But in the past fifteen years or so, many markets have started to carry pork from Berkshire hogs, which are an old-fashioned breed first raised in England. You may also find it labeled with the Japanese word *kurobuta*. It is well marbled, which makes for more tender and moist meat. Pan-roasting a double-cut chop produces perfect results. It is best served on the pink, slightly medium side of medium-rare. In the old days, hog-killing time was in the winter, when it was easier to preserve meat from spoiling and when summer and autumn's vegetables were long gone but red cabbage and apples were still fine. They are a traditional and lovely partner to these chops.

SERVES 4

FOR THE SWEET-AND-SOUR CABBAGE

2 tablespoons (30 g) unsalted butter

1 head red cabbage, shredded

1 green apple, peeled, cored, and thinly sliced

½ cup packed (110 g) light brown sugar

½ cup (120 ml) sherry vinegar

2 tablespoons whole-grain mustard

1 teaspoon kosher salt

FOR THE PORK CHOPS

2 double-cut pork chops

Kosher salt and freshly ground black pepper

1 tablespoon (15 g) unsalted butter

1. Make the sweet-and-sour cabbage: Warm the butter in a 10-inch (25 cm) nonreactive skillet over medium heat until it foams. Add the cabbage and apple and cook until the cabbage begins to soften, about 5 minutes.

2. Reduce the heat to medium-low and stir in the brown sugar, vinegar, mustard, and salt. Cook, stirring from time to time, until the cabbage turns dark red and the mixture is slightly sticky, about 45 minutes. (You can prepare the cabbage ahead of time and refrigerate it until you are ready to finish the recipe. If you do make it earlier, bring the mixture back to room temperature before you stuff the pork chops.)

3. Prepare the pork chops: Season both sides of the pork chops with salt and refrigerate for at least 2 hours. Remove the pork chops from the refrigerator 30 minutes before cooking.

4. Preheat the oven to 350°F (180°C).

5. Pat the pork chops dry and, using a paring knife, slit a pocket in the side of each pork chop, making sure not to cut all the way through. Put your fingers inside the pocket and work it open a little more. Your goal is a pocket about 2½ inches (6.5 cm) deep. Stuff ¼ cup (60 g) of the cabbage mixture into each pocket. Grind pepper over both sides of the pork chops.

6. Melt the butter in a large cast-iron skillet over medium heat until it foams. Transfer the pork chops to the skillet and place another cast-iron pan (or something of similar weight) on top of the pork chops. The pressure of the weight will produce a more uniform sear on the chops. Cook the chops until golden brown, 5 to 8 minutes per side. When the chops are nicely golden, remove the weight, transfer the pork chops to a cutting board, and check the internal temperature. If more cooking is needed, place the pork chops on a rack in a roasting pan and roast in the oven for a few minutes until they reach 125°F (52°C). Remove the chops from the oven and rest them on a cutting board for 5 to 10 minutes.

7. To serve, slice the pork off the bone and serve on top of the remaining sweet-and-sour cabbage.

PORK BELLY SLIDERS ON ANADAMA BUNS

In October, when the maple trees start to change color and it's apple-picking time, we'll often make a big fire on the beach, press a few gallons of apple cider, and serve up these sliders. They are the most delicious sandwiches ever.

MAKES 10 TO 12 SLIDERS

FOR THE MISO PORK BELLY

- ½ cup (120 g) white miso paste
- 1 cup (240 ml) apple cider
- ⅓ cup (80 ml) sake
- 2 tablespoons mirin
- 2 tablespoons rice vinegar
- 1 (2-inch/5 cm) piece fresh ginger, peeled and thinly sliced
- 2 pounds (900 g) skinless pork belly
- 1 tablespoon grapeseed or canola oil

FOR THE SLAW

- 3 apples
- ¼ head green cabbage
- 2 celery ribs
- ¼ cup (60 g) Grilled Lemon Aioli (page 307) or mayonnaise
- 2 tablespoons stone-ground mustard
- 1 shallot, minced
- 2 teaspoons kosher salt
- 1 teaspoon maple syrup

ingredients continue

1. Prepare the pork belly: In a food processor or blender, combine the miso, cider, sake, mirin, vinegar, and ginger and blend until smooth. Place the pork belly in a 1-gallon (3.84 L) zip-top plastic bag or sealable container, add the marinade, and refrigerate overnight.

2. Preheat the oven to 325°F (160°C).

3. Reserving the marinade, remove the pork belly from the bag and pat dry with paper towels. Warm the oil in a Dutch oven over medium heat until it shimmers. Sear the pork belly on each side until golden brown, about 5 minutes.

4. Transfer the pork to a cutting board and pour the fat off the pan, then return the pork to the Dutch oven along with the reserved marinade. Cover and transfer to the oven.

5. Braise until the meat is very tender, about 3 hours.

6. Remove the pork from the oven and let it rest in the braising liquid until ready to serve. If time allows, refrigerate the pork (it will be easier to slice cold).

7. Make the slaw: Peel and core the apples. Using the shredding disc on a food processor or a box grater, coarsely shred the apples, cabbage, and celery and add them to a colander. Using your hands, squeeze the apples and vegetables over the sink to release some of their water. Then transfer the vegetables to a bowl. Add the aioli, mustard, shallot, salt, and maple syrup and mix well. Set the slaw aside or refrigerate until you are ready to use it.

recipe continues

FOR SERVING

4 tablespoons (60 g/½ stick) unsalted butter, at room temperature

10 to 12 Anadama Buns (page 180) or store-bought slider buns

¼ cup (13 g) celery leaves (optional)

8. When ready to serve: Remove the pork belly from the braising liquid and slice the meat into strips ½ inch (13 mm) thick and about 3 inches (7.5 cm) long. Reserve the braising liquid.

9. Line a plate with paper towels and set it near the stove. Sear the sliced pork belly in a dry skillet over medium-high heat until golden-brown and lightly charred on the edges, about 1 minute. Flip the slices and cook for another minute. Remove the pork to the paper towels. Pour the reserved braising liquid into the skillet and deglaze it, scraping up any tasty browned bits. Set aside.

10. To serve: Warm the butter in a large nonreactive skillet over medium-high heat until it foams. Slice the Anadama buns in half horizontally and place them, cut side down, in the pan until they are nicely toasted, about 2 minutes. Remove the buns to a plate.

11. Dollop 2 tablespoons of the slaw on the bottom of each bun, place 2 slices of pork belly on top of the slaw, drizzle a spoonful of braising liquid over the pork belly, and garnish with celery leaves, if desired. Then put the top bun in place and serve.

COFFEE-RUBBED RIBS WITH BLACK BEAN SAUCE

I've been serving ribs at my Fourth of July beach barbecue for as long as I have lived on Deer Isle. Every experienced rib maker has their own special—often secret—combination of ingredients for rubs and sauces. Pretty much all of them check the boxes for sweet, salty, tangy, and even bitter. Throw in some umami to boost all those other tastes (that would be the fermented black beans in this recipe) and you're good to go. I get the special coffee that I use in the rub from 44 North in Deer Isle Village. I apply the rub the day before cooking and store the ribs in the refrigerator to let the rub do its magic. If you're pressed for time, apply the rub at least 2 hours before.

SERVES 4

FOR THE RIBS

½ cup packed (110 g) dark brown sugar

1 tablespoon kosher salt

1 tablespoon freshly ground black pepper

1 tablespoon smoked paprika

1½ teaspoons garlic powder

1½ teaspoons onion powder

1½ teaspoons mustard powder

1 teaspoon finely ground coffee

1 teaspoon Old Bay seasoning (see Notes)

1 teaspoon cayenne pepper, or to taste

2 racks baby back ribs

ingredients continue

1. Prepare the ribs: In a small food processor or blender, combine the brown sugar, salt, black pepper, smoked paprika, garlic powder, onion powder, mustard powder, ground coffee, Old Bay, and cayenne and blend until the mixture is uniform. Rub the mixture into both sides of the ribs, cover, and refrigerate overnight or at least 2 hours before roasting.

2. Make the black bean sauce: Warm the oil in a medium saucepan over medium heat until it shimmers. Add the onion and cook, stirring from time to time, until they soften and begin to char, 7 to 10 minutes.

3. Add the butter and garlic and cook for 1 minute. Add the bourbon and deglaze the pan, scraping up any browned bits from the bottom. Stir in the ketchup, brown sugar, vinegar, pepper flakes, smoked paprika, cumin, and ginger. Reduce the heat to a simmer, add the fermented black beans, and continue to stir. The sauce will come together quickly, within about 2 minutes, and it will have a slushy consistency.

4. Transfer the mixture to a blender and blend, starting at a slower speed so as not to spatter and then increasing the speed,

FOR THE BLACK BEAN SAUCE

- 1 tablespoon grapeseed or canola oil
- 1 medium onion, roughly chopped
- 1 tablespoon (15 g) unsalted butter
- 2 garlic cloves, minced
- ½ cup (120 ml) bourbon
- ¼ cup (60 ml) ketchup
- 2 tablespoons dark brown sugar
- 1 tablespoon red wine vinegar
- ½ teaspoon red pepper flakes
- ½ teaspoon smoked paprika
- ¼ teaspoon ground cumin
- ¼ teaspoon ground ginger
- ⅓ cup (60 g) fermented black beans (see Notes)

FOR SERVING

- 2 tablespoons minced fresh flat-leaf parsley
- 2 tablespoons minced fresh chives

until completely smooth. If the sauce is too thick for the blender to do its work, loosen it with a tablespoon or two of water.

5. Preheat the oven to 300°F (150°C).

6. Place the ribs in a roasting pan, bone side down. Cover the pan with foil and cook the ribs in the oven until tender and the meat is falling off the bone, about 2 hours. Remove the pan from the oven (see Notes).

7. Increase the oven temperature to 425°F (220°C). Slather the black bean sauce on the ribs. When the oven reaches the desired temperature, return the ribs to the oven, uncovered, and bake for 5 minutes so that the black bean coating firms up a bit.

8. To serve: Place the ribs on a platter, separate them with a chef's knife, and garnish with the parsley and chives.

NOTES: Old Bay seasoning is a widely available mix of herbs and spices, originally made to be boiled with the shrimp and crabs of the Chesapeake Bay. You can use it pretty much anywhere you want a ready-made herb and spice mix.

You can find fermented black beans in Asian markets, many supermarkets, and online.

When the ribs have finished their initial roasting, they can be refrigerated and finished later. Remove them from the refrigerator about 30 minutes before serving, then proceed as above, slathering on the black bean sauce and finishing the ribs in a 425°F (220°C) oven for 5 minutes.

BRAISED SHORT RIBS AND WILD RAMP PANCAKES

Spring arrives in Maine in fits and starts. I like to make this recipe on a chilly day in April when spring has not made up its mind to play nice. Short ribs, marinated for a long time and then slowly braised, are about as stick-to-your-ribs and scrumptious as anything you can cook. Ramps (also known as wild leeks) grow all over the eastern part of the US. Their green shoots first sprout when sunlight warms the forest's carpet of moss and pine needles. Raw ramps are sharp as raw onions, but, like onions, they sweeten when cooked.

SERVES 4 TO 6

FOR THE SHORT RIBS

2 cups (480 ml) tamari

¾ cup (150 g) sugar

6 garlic cloves, smashed

1 (2-inch/5 cm) piece fresh ginger, peeled and minced or grated

2 tablespoons toasted sesame oil

1 tablespoon red pepper flakes, or to taste

4 bone-in short ribs

2 cups (480 ml) Roasted Chicken Stock (page 305) or store-bought beef stock

FOR THE RAMP CAKES

3 cups (375 g) all-purpose flour, plus more for dusting

¾ teaspoon kosher salt

¾ cup (180 ml) boiling water

2 tablespoons cool water, as needed

ingredients continue

1. Prepare the short ribs: In a food processor or blender, combine the tamari, sugar, garlic, ginger, sesame oil, and pepper flakes. Blend briefly until smooth, scraping down the sides with a rubber spatula, if necessary. Pour the marinade over the short ribs in a covered container or a 1-gallon (3.84 L) zip-top plastic bag and refrigerate for at least 3 hours and preferably overnight.

2. Preheat the oven to 325°F (160°C).

3. In a nonreactive Dutch oven, place the short ribs, stock, and enough marinade to come halfway up the sides of the short ribs. (Discard the remaining marinade.) Cover and braise in the oven until the short ribs are fork-tender and pull away easily from the bone, about 2½ hours.

4. Remove the short ribs from the braising liquid and set them aside until they are cool enough to handle, then use your hands to shred the meat and discard the bones. Strain the braising liquid and add ¼ to ½ cup (60 to 120 ml) to the shredded meat so that it is well moistened. Discard all but 1 cup (240 ml) of the strained braising liquid.

5. Make the ramp cakes: In a large bowl, combine the flour and salt. Pour in the boiling water and mix with a wooden spoon until the water is fully absorbed. As needed, add 1 tablespoon of cool water at a time until the dough comes together completely and all

12 medium ramps (see Notes)

Toasted sesame oil, for brushing

⅓ cup (80 ml) grapeseed or canola oil

FOR SERVING

Pickled Red Onions (page 316; optional)

Fresh cilantro leaves or other herb of your choice

the flour is incorporated. Turn the dough out onto a work surface lightly dusted with flour. Knead the dough until a firm ball is formed, about 5 minutes. Place the dough in a bowl, cover with a clean kitchen towel, and set aside to rest for 20 minutes.

6. Cut off the leaves of the ramps and save them for another use (see Notes). Slice the bottoms of the ramps crosswise into ¼-inch (6 mm) slices and set aside.

7. Preheat the oven to its lowest setting and place a baking sheet on the middle rack.

8. Divide the dough in half. Using a rolling pin, roll out each piece of dough into a roughly shaped rectangle ¼ inch (6 mm) thick and about 12 inches (30 cm) long. Brush each rolled-out dough with sesame oil and scatter liberally with the ramps. Starting with the long side, roll each rectangle into a log. Slice each log crosswise into six 2-inch-wide (5 cm) pieces. Turn the slices cut side up and cup each one with your hands to lightly press the swirls together. Gently flatten each slice with a rolling pin to produce a pancake about 5 inches (13 cm) in diameter.

9. Warm 2 tablespoons of the grapeseed oil in a large skillet over medium-high heat until it shimmers. Working in batches, add the ramp cakes and fry until they are golden brown on one side, about 2 minutes. Flip and cook until golden on the other side, another 2 minutes. As each batch of ramp cakes is done, place the cooked cakes on the baking sheet in the oven. Add more oil as needed to cook the remaining ramp cakes so that you always keep some sizzle going as the cakes fry.

10. To serve: Place 2 or 3 ramp cakes on each dinner plate and top with a dollop of the moistened shredded meat. Spoon a tablespoon of the strained braising liquid over the meat. If desired, garnish with pickled red onion and cilantro, then serve.

NOTES: If you don't have ramps, you can use scallions.

Save the ramp greens for making a compound butter (see page 171) or the sauce for Scallops with Wild Ramp Sauce (page 96).

VENISON TENDERLOIN

Maine has a thriving population of white-tailed deer and many enthusiastic deer hunters. On frosty autumn mornings, the early stillness is broken, from time to time, with the echo of rifle fire. Then the yearly ritual begins: sausage making, the preparation of the family's secret venison chili, and—my favorite way to mark a successful hunt—spice-crusted venison tenderloin, roasted medium-rare, full of the flavor of the Maine woods.

SERVES 4

FOR THE VENISON

1½ pounds (680 g) venison tenderloin

1 cup (240 ml) red wine

1 medium shallot, finely diced

2 garlic cloves, smashed

2 thyme sprigs

2 tablespoons grapeseed or canola oil

FOR THE SAUCE

1 medium beet, peeled, quartered, and boiled until soft (about 20 minutes)

1 cup (240 ml) chicken stock, homemade (page 305) or store-bought

4 teaspoons red wine vinegar

1 tablespoon juniper berries

1 bay leaf

3 tablespoons (45 g) unsalted butter, cubed

Kosher salt

1. Marinate the venison: Place the venison in a zip-top bag or container with a lid and add the wine, shallot, garlic, and thyme. Marinate the venison in the refrigerator for at least 2 hours or up to 24 hours. If the venison is not completely covered by the marinade, make sure to flip it halfway through.

2. Remove the venison from the marinade (reserve the marinade for the sauce) and pat it dry with a paper towels. Let the venison come to room temperature, about 1 hour, before cooking.

3. Preheat the oven to 375°F (190°C).

4. Make the sauce: Using a blender or small food processor, puree the boiled beet with 2 tablespoons of the chicken stock. Transfer the puree to a small saucepan and add the remaining chicken stock, the reserved marinade, the vinegar, juniper berries, and bay leaf. Bring to a vigorous simmer over medium-low heat, then cook until the liquid has reduced by half, 15 to 20 minutes. Strain the liquid using a fine-mesh strainer and return it to the pan. Over low heat, whisk in the butter, one cube at a time, until all the butter is fully incorporated. Remove from the heat. Taste the sauce and season with salt.

5. Make the spice crust: Grind or crush the peppercorns and juniper berries in a spice grinder or using a mortar and pestle. Combine the spices with the salt. Spread the mixture on a cutting board. Slather the venison with enough Dijon mustard to lightly coat it, and then press both sides of the venison into the spice mixture.

FOR THE SPICE CRUST

1 tablespoon whole black peppercorns

1 tablespoon juniper berries

2 teaspoons kosher salt

1 tablespoon Dijon mustard, plus more as needed

6. Cook the venison: Warm the oil in a large skillet over medium-high heat until it shimmers. Add the venison and sear for 2 minutes per side. Transfer the venison to a rack set in a roasting pan. Roast for about 7 minutes, until the meat reaches an internal temperature of 120°F (48°C). (The cooking time will vary depending on the thickness of the meat.) Remove the venison from the oven and set it aside to rest while you rewarm the sauce.

7. Slice the venison into ½-inch-thick (13 mm) slices and place it on a platter. Spoon the sauce over the tenderloin and serve. Store any leftovers in an airtight container in the refrigerator for up to 4 days.

DOWNEAST
MUSHROOMS
GROWN ON DEER ISLE MAINE

VEGETABLES

You'd be hard pressed to taste vegetables that are more bursting with flavor than those that grow within a short drive of Goose Cove. Part of the explanation for this, I am told, is that Maine lies farther north than the rest of the lower forty-eight, so we have more precious minutes of sunlight in the growing season. Then there is the fact that ocean water has a moderating effect on air temperature, so, although our fields and orchards wake up a bit later in the spring, by the time they are ready to start growing, ripening, and soaking up the abundant sun of warm days, there is little chance of a killing frost.

The main reason, though, that our fruits and vegetables have such spectacular taste is that our farmers are amazing stewards of the land, constantly enriching it, taking advantage of nature's gifts. Much of this owes to the work of Eliot Coleman, who is widely celebrated as the father of modern organic gardening. When he was a young man, Eliot read a book called *Living the Good Life* by Helen and Scott Nearing. Like generations of big-city dwellers before them, the Nearings felt the attraction of a simpler pace of living in rural New England. Setting up a homestead in Vermont, they decided to live completely off the grid and to raise their food organically. Helen and Scott subsequently left Vermont for Maine. When Eliot read their book in the 1960s, he was captivated and showed up at their doorstep and said, "Put me to work."

They did.

In time, the Nearings saw that young Eliot had a super green thumb and a natural understanding of how to farm sustainably and—very important—to achieve maximum flavor. After a few years, they offered Eliot 60 acres of rocky, uncleared evergreen forest at $33 per acre. Eliot thrived on his new land that he named Four Season Farm. He was determined to reap the land's bounty through all four seasons and invented an ingenious way of extending the growing season by utilizing low-cost, low-tech greenhouses so that he could give his plants an extra dose of warmth as the cycle of seasons progressed. By recycling, composting, and rotating crops, Eliot has turned his hardscrabble Maine soil into rich topsoil. Flavor, Eliot says, begins in the ground. I totally agree; you can't make great meals without great ingredients.

Where Eliot led, others have followed, picking up the banner of seasonal, organic sustainability. Missy Greene's Yellow Birch Farm, just down the road from me, produces great fruits and vegetables as well as fine cheeses, courtesy of her herd of goats that live off the leavings of her garden. Across Penobscot Bay, Hubert McCabe and Sarah Tompkins's Fine Line Farm provides the tenderest and most delicious baby vegetables. Their motto pretty much sums up the credo of our dedicated local farmers: "No herbicides, no pesticides, no fungicides, and no chemical fertilizers. Not now. Not ever!"

RATATOUILLE CASSEROLE

There comes an enchanted time each summer when just about every plant in the garden is shouting, "Pick me!" Here is a way to gather many vegetables in one delicious recipe. Basically, it's a ratatouille in which all the vegetables are arranged in luscious rings on top of a puree of roasted pepper, onion, garlic, tomatillo, and fresh herbs. When the vegetable rounds are piled up and laid in a baking dish with the edges facing up, they look like stacks of poker chips. When the ratatouille comes out of the oven, the rustic but orderly design is a real showstopper. Serve it hot or cold, and have a crusty baguette or country bread to mop up the juices. You can also serve ratatouille as a side dish with roast lamb or a steak.

MAKES ONE 10-INCH (25 CM) ROUND CASSEROLE

FOR THE VEGETABLE PUREE

2 red bell peppers, quartered

2 tomatillos, husked and quartered

1 yellow onion, roughly chopped

5 garlic cloves, peeled

3 tablespoons olive oil

1 teaspoon kosher salt

¼ cup (60 ml) Roasted Vegetable Stock (page 302), Roasted Chicken Stock (page 305), or store-bought stock

¼ cup (9 g) chopped fresh oregano

2 tablespoons chopped fresh flat-leaf parsley

2 tablespoons sherry vinegar

1. Make the vegetable puree: Preheat the oven to 375°F (190°C).

2. In a medium bowl, combine the bell peppers, tomatillos, onion, and garlic. Add the olive oil and salt and toss to coat. Arrange the vegetables on a baking sheet and transfer to the oven.

3. Roast the vegetables until they are lightly charred, about 30 minutes. Remove the vegetables from the oven and transfer to a food processor or blender. Add a splash of stock, if needed.

4. Starting at a slower speed so as not to spatter and then increasing the speed, blend until completely smooth. If needed, add a bit more stock to get the mixture moving. Add the oregano, parsley, and vinegar and blend for 10 to 15 seconds. The puree should have the consistency of applesauce.

5. Meanwhile, make the vegetable "poker chips": Set out four bowls, one for each vegetable (assembling the ratatouille will go faster if you keep the vegetables separate). Using a mandoline or very sharp knife, carefully slice the eggplants, summer squash, and zucchini into rounds about ¼ inch (6 mm) thick. Use a serrated knife to slice the tomatoes. Place each vegetable in its own bowl. Season each vegetable with a bit of salt. Set the vegetables aside for 20 minutes so that the salt extracts some water.

FOR THE VEGETABLE "POKER CHIPS" (SEE NOTE)

3 Japanese eggplants
2 medium summer squash
2 medium zucchini
4 medium tomatoes
6 tablespoons (108 g) kosher salt, plus more as needed
8 large basil leaves
1 tablespoon olive oil

FOR SERVING

2 tablespoons thinly sliced fresh basil leaves
Crusty bread

6. Line two baking sheets with paper towels and set them near your work surface. Drain the eggplant, squash, and zucchini and lay them out in a single layer on the prepared baking sheets. Salt the tomatoes a bit more and lay them out in a single layer on one of the baking sheets. Set the vegetables aside for 30 minutes, allowing them to drain off more moisture.

7. When you are ready to proceed, preheat the oven to 325°F (160°C).

8. Pat the vegetables with fresh paper towels to pick up additional moisture. To assemble the ingredients, spread the puree evenly on the bottom of a 10-inch (25 cm) round casserole dish. Next, stack the vegetables, alternating eggplant, squash, zucchini, and tomato (see photos, page 209). When you have about 8 slices in a stack, gently squeeze the stack to remove even more moisture, then transfer the stack to the casserole dish, layering the vegetable slices with their edges facing up. As you assemble each stack, continue to place it in the casserole dish until you have completed a circle or two. Tuck basil leaves in between the stacks. Fill the center of the circle with a shorter stack. Sprinkle a few dashes of salt over the top of the casserole, drizzle with the olive oil, and cover with foil.

9. Transfer to the oven and bake for 30 minutes. Remove the foil and continue to bake until the vegetables are lightly caramelized and softened and the ratatouille is gently bubbling, about 1 hour. Let the casserole rest for 10 minutes before serving.

10. To serve: Garnish the casserole with the sliced basil and present the casserole on a trivet or hot pad. Serve in wide soup plates with crusty bread alongside. Any leftovers can be stored in an airtight container in the refrigerator for 3 to 4 days.

NOTE: Look for eggplants, summer squash, zucchini, and tomatoes that are about the same diameter, 2 to 3 inches (5 to 7.5 cm). You can always slice larger vegetable rounds in half.

SQUASH BLOSSOMS STUFFED WITH CRAB SALAD

The orange and yellow color of a squash blossom looks like a flicker of a flame on top of a slender green candle. When zucchini are ready to ripen in August and September, their flowers are just right for picking and stuffing. Early in my career, when I cooked in Italy for a houseful of American tourists, I first came across deep-fried squash flowers filled with a creamy mascarpone-based mixture. In Maine, I stuff them with crab salad. The happy result is crispy, delicate, warm, and savory. Nobody ever eats just one. Serve them as people stand around in your kitchen having an aperitif or pass them around at a cocktail party on a canapé tray. My beverage choice would be a glass of a cold crisp white wine or a dry champagne.

SERVES 4 AS AN APPETIZER OR LIGHT MAIN COURSE

FOR THE STUFFING

1 pound (455 g) backfin crabmeat (see Note, page 61)

½ cup (115 g) mascarpone

1 celery rib, medium-diced

1 medium shallot, finely diced

Grated zest and juice of 1 lemon

2 tablespoons chopped fresh dill

1½ teaspoons kosher salt

1 teaspoon Aleppo pepper

FOR THE BATTER

½ cup (65 g) all-purpose flour

ingredients continue

1. Make the stuffing: In a large bowl, combine the crabmeat, mascarpone, celery, shallot, lemon zest, lemon juice, dill, salt, and Aleppo pepper. Set aside.

2. Make the batter: In a medium bowl, combine the flour, cornstarch, baking powder, and salt. Pour in the sparkling water, a little at a time, stirring until the batter is smooth.

3. To cook: Check the squash blossoms to make sure they are clean and free of dirt and insects. Trim the stems of the squash blossoms, leaving about 3 inches (7.5 cm) below the blossoms. Spread the petals of each blossom, and pinch and discard the stamen. Using a spoon or a piping bag, fill each blossom with the crab salad, leaving 1 inch (2.5 cm) at the top unfilled. Gently twist the top of each blossom until it comes together; you might try wetting your fingers for this step (see photos, page 213).

4. Line a plate with paper towels and set it near the stove. Warm the oil in a deep saucepan to 350°F (180°C) or until the oil bubbles when you insert a wooden spoon.

recipe continues

½ cup (65 g) cornstarch
1 tablespoon baking powder
1 teaspoon kosher salt
1½ cups (360 ml) sparkling water

FOR COOKING

12 large squash blossoms, cleaned (see Note)
4 cups (960 ml) grapeseed or canola oil, plus more as needed
Kosher salt

5. Working in batches to avoid overcrowding, hold a blossom by the stem, dip it in the batter, and then lift it out, allowing any excess batter to drain for a second. Gently lower it into the hot oil. Fry the blossoms until they are lightly golden all over, 2 to 3 minutes. Remove them to the paper towels to drain and lightly salt them. Let the blossoms cool for 5 minutes before passing them around.

NOTE: Whenever you use flowers in a recipe, make sure they have not been treated with pesticides. To clean, gently rinse them and pat dry with a paper towel.

FARM SALAD

Although I love a simple salad of greens and vinaigrette, sometimes it's more fun for the salad maker, and the eater, when the salad offers a surprise. This salad incorporates a base layer of roasted beets, ricotta, pickled mushrooms, and dukkah, a North African spice mix. You'll cover the layer with delicate dressed greens—the younger the better—and, to make it extra special, top the salad with nasturtium leaves and flowers. The vegetables are revealed as you dig down through the greens and flowers.

SERVES 4

4 medium beets, scrubbed
1 tablespoon grapeseed or canola oil
Kosher salt
Grated zest of ½ lemon
1½ teaspoons fresh lemon juice
Freshly ground black pepper

FOR THE VINAIGRETTE

½ medium shallot, finely diced
1 tablespoon Dijon mustard
1 tablespoon sherry vinegar
½ teaspoon kosher salt
2 tablespoons good-quality olive oil

FOR THE SALAD

1 cup (245 g) ricotta cheese
Grated zest of ½ lemon
1½ teaspoons fresh lemon juice

1. Preheat the oven to 400°F (200°C).

2. Place each beet on a separate piece of aluminum foil. Drizzle with oil and sprinkle liberally with salt. Wrap the beets in the foil and bake on a baking sheet until fork-tender, about 50 minutes. Test for doneness by inserting a skewer or cake tester into a beet. The beets are done when you can penetrate them easily.

3. Carefully unwrap the beets and set them aside until they are cool enough to handle, about 10 minutes. Using paper towels or a dish rag, rub the skin off the warm beets and slice into wedges. Place the beets in a bowl, toss with the lemon zest and juice, season with salt and pepper, and set aside.

4. Meanwhile, make the vinaigrette: In a small bowl, whisk together the shallot, mustard, vinegar, and salt. Drizzle in the olive oil while whisking until fully emulsified. Set the dressing aside.

5. Make the salad: In a small bowl, mix together the ricotta, lemon zest, and lemon juice. Spoon ¼ cup (60 g) of the ricotta mix onto each plate and, using a tablespoon or a serving spoon, press down on each mound of ricotta to make a little well. Place the beet wedges and the pickled mushrooms in the ricotta wells and sprinkle with dukkah.

½ cup (130 g) Pickled Shimeji Mushrooms (page 317)

1 teaspoon Dukkah (recipe follows)

1 pound (455 g) mesclun or mixed baby greens

8 nasturtium leaves and flowers, for garnish (optional; see Note)

6. In a large bowl, toss the mesclun with the vinaigrette. Cover the ricotta/beet/mushroom mounds with the dressed mesclun. If desired, garnish with nasturtium leaves and flowers.

NOTE: Whenever you use flowers in a recipe, make sure they haven't been treated with pesticides. To clean, gently rinse them and pat dry with a paper towel.

Dukkah

MAKES ABOUT 1¼ CUPS (180 G)

½ cup (80 g) cracked oats

¼ cup (30 g) raw pumpkin seeds

¼ cup (35 g) raw sunflower seeds

¼ cup (30 g) fennel seeds

1 teaspoon coriander seeds

1 teaspoon cumin seeds

1 teaspoon flaxseeds

1 teaspoon kosher salt

½ teaspoon cayenne pepper

Dukkah is a mix of nuts and seeds from North Africa that lends crunch and notes of aromatic spice as a finishing garnish for many recipes. It's great on salads but also nice on fish, roast chicken, and baked potatoes. Try it on your favorite dishes; it's pretty all-purpose.

In a small dry skillet, combine the oats, pumpkin seeds, sunflower seeds, fennel seeds, coriander seeds, cumin seeds, and flaxseeds and toast over medium heat for a few minutes. As soon as you smell a spicy, nutty aroma, transfer the mixture to a small food processor or a mortar and pestle. Add the salt and cayenne and process to a coarse grind. You can use the mix immediately or store it in an airtight container at room temperature for up to 2 weeks.

5.31
GB

TOMATO GALETTE

Hats off to my mom here. Every year, at the peak of summer, she makes her tomato pie. Actually, it's a galette, which is a pie with a free-form crust, which is much less fussy than a regular piecrust. The key to this recipe is taking the time to prep the main ingredients. Before adding the cherry tomatoes to the filling, roast them until they start to burst. You also want to caramelize the onions. If anybody tells you they can caramelize onions in 10 minutes, don't believe it. Caramelizing onions over low heat, frequently stirring them and scraping up the browned bits of the gently sizzling onions, is the only way to get deeply sweet, uniformly caramelized onions. It should take about 30 minutes and requires your attention to keep the onions from scorching. The transformation is magical and well worth the extra effort. Topping the galette with crumbled feta adds a touch of creaminess and acidity and creates a beautiful visual contrast as well.

SERVES 4
AS A LIGHT MAIN COURSE

FOR THE CRUST

1 cup (125 g) all-purpose flour

½ teaspoon kosher salt

8 tablespoons (115 g/1 stick) cold unsalted butter

¼ cup (60 ml) cold water, as needed

FOR THE FILLING

1 pound (455 g) cherry tomatoes

2 tablespoons olive oil

Kosher salt

2 tablespoons (30 g) unsalted butter

3 medium red onions, thinly sliced

ingredients continue

1. Make the crust: In a large bowl, combine the flour and salt. Using a box grater, grate in the cold butter and mix by hand to incorporate it. Take care not to overwork it because you want the butter to remain in pea-size pieces. Add the cold water slowly and mix until the dough barely comes together. It will be shaggy; no kneading needed. Cover the dough and let rest in the refrigerator for 30 minutes.

2. Make the filling: Preheat the oven to 300°F (150°C).

3. In a bowl, toss the cherry tomatoes with the olive oil and 1 teaspoon salt. Then spread them out on a baking sheet. Roast the tomatoes in the oven until they are starting to burst, about 1 hour. Check on them from time to time, giving the pan a few shakes to roll them around.

4. Meanwhile, warm the butter in a large skillet over medium-low heat until it foams. Add the onions and a pinch of salt. Cook the onions until they caramelize and turn dark brown, stirring often to avoid burning, about 30 minutes. Remove the onions from the skillet and set aside in a small bowl.

recipe continues

¼ cup (50 g) sugar

1 tablespoon maple syrup

1 tablespoon sherry vinegar

FOR ASSEMBLY

All-purpose flour, for dusting

2 tablespoons crumbled feta cheese

Egg wash: 1 large egg beaten with 1 tablespoon milk

5. In a small saucepan, combine the sugar and 2 tablespoons water and warm over medium heat until it takes on an amber color, about 5 minutes. Gently swirl the pan so that the sugar fully dissolves. As the water evaporates, the bubbles will get bigger and the liquid will thicken.

6. Add the maple syrup and cook for 1 minute. Add the vinegar, carefully to avoid spatter, and continue to cook for about 1 minute to thoroughly warm. Remove the pan from the heat and set the maple-vinegar mixture aside.

7. Remove the tomatoes from the oven and increase the oven temperature to 400°F (200°C). Line a baking sheet with parchment paper.

8. To assemble: On a floured work surface, roll out the dough into a rough round ⅛ inch (3 mm) thick. Place a 12-inch (30 cm) dinner plate upside down on the dough, lightly pressing down so that the dinner plate leaves its outline in the dough when you remove the plate. Set the plate aside and make six 1-inch (2.5 cm) slits around the edge of the rough round. Transfer the dough to the lined baking sheet.

9. Place the caramelized onions in the center of the rolled-out dough and, using a spatula, spread the onion mixture evenly, leaving about 1 inch (2.5 cm) of the circular pattern you traced with the dinner plate as a border (which will allow for neatly folding the dough where you've created the slits). Spread the tomatoes over the onions and drizzle the maple-vinegar mixture over the tomatoes. Top with the feta. Fold the fringed edges of the dough over to enclose the galette. Brush the crust of the galette with the egg wash.

10. Bake for 25 minutes. The crust should be nicely golden (it may need another minute or two in the oven to achieve this color).

11. Let the galette cool for at least 20 minutes on a wire rack, then transfer the galette to a flat surface or cutting board. Slice it into pie-shaped wedges and serve. Any leftovers can be stored in an airtight container in the refrigerator for 3 to 4 days.

SCORCHED VEGETABLES WITH FISH CARAMEL

Fish caramel is one of my kitchen staples, a powerhouse potion of brown sugar, fish sauce, lime juice, maple syrup, Thai chiles, and ginger. It has a good bit of umami from the fish sauce, which gives a major flavor boost to anything you pair it with. I often use it as a finishing touch for scorched vegetables—whatever is in season. If you happen to have any leftover fish caramel, try it on sliced steak, grilled quail, all kinds of tempura, seared scallops, or grilled shrimp.

Using a grill basket is the best way to grill vegetables so that they don't fall through the grates or roll off the grill. Whether you are cooking over live fire or charcoal, on a gas grill, or on a ridged grill pan on a stovetop, taste the vegetables for doneness. They are done when they taste right to you—scorched but not burnt, still crispy but not raw.

SERVES 8 TO 10

Grapeseed or canola oil, for the grill

FOR THE VEGETABLES

Fresh vegetables of your choice (you can easily do a couple of pounds of carrots, string beans, Brussels sprouts, or cauliflower or a few heads of lettuce or radicchio; see Note)

Fish Caramel (recipe follows), for serving

Furikake, homemade (page 149) or store-bought, for sprinkling (optional)

1. Prepare an outdoor grill to medium-high heat or, if cooking inside, preheat a ridged grill pan over medium-high heat for a few minutes. For a charcoal grill, the fire is ready when you can hold your hand 4 inches (10 cm) above the grate for a full 3 seconds before it feels too hot. For a gas grill, turn it to high a few minutes before cooking the vegetables.

2. Just before cooking the vegetables, brush the grill grate or ridged grill pan with a lightly oiled paper towel. Place the vegetables in a grill basket and set the basket over the grill grate. If using a ridged grill pan, the vegetables can go directly on the grill pan. Charring time for the vegetables depends on how hot your fire is. Remember to flip the grill basket a few times during cooking. Over medium-high heat, dense vegetables such as carrots or Brussels sprouts can take 10 minutes to cook and develop a nice char. Vegetables such as snap peas, string beans, or Broccolini take 5 to 7 minutes. Sturdy leafy vegetables such as chard or kale take 3 to 4 minutes, and tender leafy vegetables such as romaine lettuce, Little Gems, or radicchio are done after

2 to 3 minutes. Adjust the cook times to your taste and bear in mind that grilled vegetables should still have a little crunch.

3. Transfer the grilled vegetables to a platter and pour enough fish caramel over the vegetables to coat them lightly. Sprinkle with furikake, if desired, and serve.

NOTE: Hardier vegetables, such as carrots, Brussels sprouts, string beans, and cauliflower should be blanched for a few minutes to tenderize them before grilling.

Fish Caramel

MAKES ABOUT
2 CUPS (480 ML)

- 1½ cups packed (330 g) dark brown sugar
- ¾ cup (180 ml) Thai fish sauce
- ½ cup (120 ml) maple syrup
- 1 leek, halved lengthwise, well rinsed, and thinly sliced
- 2 scallions, thinly sliced crosswise
- 1 (1-inch/2.5 cm) piece fresh ginger, peeled and medium-diced
- 2 garlic cloves, roughly chopped
- 1 or 2 fresh Thai chiles, finely diced
- 1 tablespoon fresh lime juice
- 2 tablespoons (30 g) unsalted butter

1. In a deep saucepan, combine the brown sugar, fish sauce, and maple syrup and cook over medium heat, stirring constantly, until the sugar dissolves, about 3 minutes.

2. Stir in the leek, scallions, ginger, garlic, and chile(s). Cook at a medium simmer, swirling occasionally to keep the foaming mixture from bubbling over as it thickens. Cook until a thermometer (preferably a candy thermometer) registers 235°F (113°C); in candy making this is called the soft ball stage. The caramel should be quite sticky. Remove from the heat and carefully, to avoid spattering, add the lime juice. Add the butter and, moving the pan in a circular motion, swirl in the butter or use a whisk to combine. Set aside to cool for 30 minutes. Store the fish caramel in an airtight container in the refrigerator for up to 2 weeks.

SWEET CORN VEGETARIAN CHOWDER

Chowder is as New England as a soup can be. It's usually made with clams, lobster, or finfish, but this vegetarian version is quite hearty and stick-to-your-ribs. It hits the spot when served up warm on a rainy day. Try it chilled the next day, just like cold leek-and-potato soup. Rain or shine, it makes for a lovely lunch served with a green salad and a piece of crusty bread.

SERVES 4 TO 6

- 6 scallions
- 3 tablespoons (45 g) unsalted butter
- 3 celery ribs, medium-diced
- 1 red bell pepper, roughly diced
- 1 jalapeño pepper, seeded and finely diced
- 8 ears sweet corn, kernels scraped from cobs
- 1 pound (455 g) russet potatoes, peeled and cut into ½-inch (13 mm) cubes
- 1 quart (960 ml) vegetable stock, homemade (page 302) or store-bought
- 1 cup (240 ml) whole milk
- 1 cup (240 ml) heavy cream
- 1 bay leaf
- 1 teaspoon kosher salt
- ½ teaspoon freshly ground black pepper
- ½ teaspoon ground turmeric
- Furikake, homemade (page 149) or store-bought (optional)

1. Thinly slice the scallions and set aside a few tablespoons for garnish.

2. Warm the butter in a soup pot over medium heat until it foams. Add the scallions, celery, bell pepper, and jalapeño. Cook until the vegetables start to soften, 5 to 7 minutes.

3. Set aside ¼ cup (35 g) of the corn kernels for garnish and add the remaining corn kernels to the pot. Add the potatoes, vegetable stock, milk, heavy cream, bay leaf, salt, black pepper, and turmeric. Bring to a medium simmer and cook until the potatoes are tender and pierce easily with a fork, about 10 minutes.

4. Discard the bay leaf. Transfer half the mixture to a food processor or blender. Blend, starting at a slower speed so as not to spatter and then increasing the speed, until completely smooth. Return the puree to the pot and simmer to the desired temperature for serving, usually about 5 minutes.

5. To serve, ladle the chowder into soup bowls. Garnish with the reserved corn kernels, the reserved scallions, and the furikake, if desired. Store any leftover chowder in an airtight container in the refrigerator for up to 4 days.

CANDY CARROTS WITH MOLE VERDE

Candy carrots are one of the many triumphs of Eliot Coleman's organic garden experiments (for more on his Four Season Farm, see page 203). They elevate carrots from an "eat your vegetables" obligation to a standout ingredient. If you can't find this variety, look for carrots with a high natural sugar content; you're more likely to find them at a farmers' market. The earthy sweetness of roasted carrots pairs beautifully with the mildly spicy mole verde that showcases tangy sweet tomatillos, an often overlooked but delicious ingredient.

SERVES 4

FOR THE CARROTS

1 pound (455 g) young sweet carrots, such as candy carrots

2 tablespoons extra-virgin olive oil

1 teaspoon kosher salt

FOR THE MOLE VERDE

¾ cup (100 g) raw pumpkin seeds

2 cups (480 ml) chicken stock, homemade (page 305) or store-bought

10 tomatillos, husked and halved

1 medium onion, roughly chopped

2 garlic cloves, peeled

2 serrano peppers, halved lengthwise; save the seeds from one of the peppers

1 tablespoon ground coriander

1. Roast the carrots: Preheat the oven to 400°F (200°C).

2. Using a stiff brush, scrub the carrots. Place them on a baking sheet. Add the olive oil and salt and roll the carrots around to coat them evenly. Transfer to the oven and roast until the carrots are tender, about 35 minutes. Remove the carrots to a serving platter.

3. Meanwhile, make the mole verde: In a spice grinder or mini food processor, chop or very coarsely grind the pumpkin seeds.

4. In a deep saucepan, combine the ground pumpkin seeds, chicken stock, tomatillos, onion, garlic, serranos (and seeds), coriander, and bay leaves. Cook over low heat until the vegetables are soft, about 20 minutes.

5. Set a colander over a bowl and drain the vegetables, reserving the poaching liquid in the bowl. Discard the bay leaves. Transfer the drained vegetables to a food processor or blender. Add the parsley, cilantro, oregano, lime zest, and lime juice and blend, starting at a slower speed so as not to spatter and then increasing the speed, until completely smooth. As you blend, slowly add just enough of the reserved poaching liquid to give the mole the consistency of applesauce.

2 bay leaves

1 cup (50 g) fresh flat-leaf parsley leaves

1 cup (40 g) fresh cilantro

3 oregano sprigs

Grated zest and juice of 2 limes

6. Spoon the mole over the roasted carrots and serve. Store any leftover mole in an airtight container in the refrigerator for 3 to 5 days.

GRILLED CORN SALAD WITH BLISTERED TOMATO VINAIGRETTE

Grilling vegetables over hot coals gives them a subtle smoky char and caramelization, drawing out their sweetness. Grilling will also get you out of the kitchen on a hot day (and, yes, we get hot days even in Maine). Serve this as the centerpiece of a light supper or, if you have the barbecue going, this salad goes well as a side for any grilled meat or fish. In other words, it's good as a solo act, but it also plays well with others.

SERVES 4

Grapeseed or canola oil, for the grill

FOR THE BLISTERED TOMATO VINAIGRETTE

1 pound (455 g) cherry tomatoes

2 tablespoons grapeseed or canola oil

1 medium shallot, thinly sliced

1 tablespoon sherry vinegar

Grated zest and juice of 1 lime

½ teaspoon chipotle powder, plus more to taste

½ teaspoon smoked paprika

¼ cup (60 ml) olive oil

FOR THE SALAD

4 ears sweet corn, shucked

6 garlic scapes, tough outer layer removed

4 ounces (115 g) feta cheese, roughly diced

ingredients continue

1. Prepare an outdoor grill to high heat or, if cooking inside, preheat a grill pan over high heat for a few minutes.

2. Just before cooking, oil the grill or grill pan with an oiled paper towel. A light coating of oil is all you need on the pan.

3. Make the blistered tomato vinaigrette: In a bowl, toss the tomatoes with the grapeseed oil. Place the tomatoes in a grill basket or on the grill pan and grill them for a few minutes, until they blister. If some tomatoes blacken a bit, that's fine. Remove the charred tomatoes and reserve 8 blistered tomatoes to finish the salad. Keep the grill going or the grill pan hot.

4. Transfer the rest of the tomatoes to a blender. Add the shallot, vinegar, lime zest, lime juice, chipotle powder, and smoked paprika. Blend at a slow speed to combine. Taste the mixture, and if you'd like it spicier, add more chipotle. With the blender running, add the olive oil in a slow stream until the puree has the consistency of a hearty marinara sauce. Set aside.

5. Assemble the salad: Place the corn on the grill or grill pan and use tongs to turn the corn as each side lightly chars, 3 to 4 minutes. Scrape the kernels into a bowl.

6. Char the garlic scapes over the grill or on the grill pan for just a few minutes and then set them aside. When they are cool

- 1 cucumber, peeled, seeded, and roughly diced
- 1 red bell pepper, roughly diced
- 1 tablespoon chopped fresh cilantro
- 1 tablespoon thinly sliced fresh basil
- Kosher salt

enough to handle, roughly chop the charred scapes and add them to the bowl with the corn kernels.

7. Add the reserved blistered tomatoes and the feta, cucumber, and bell pepper. Toss with just enough of the vinaigrette to coat everything (see Note). Garnish with cilantro and basil. Season to taste with salt and serve.

NOTE: This recipe may produce more vinaigrette than you need to dress the salad. Slather it on toasted bread or use it to dress most any salad, grilled fish, or leftover steak.

BACONY LEEK POTATO GRATIN

For a holiday meal or really any time, ham and potatoes make an excellent pair. The next time you serve a baked ham, try this gratin to liven up your potatoes. The gratin is super tasty and super rich and can lead to a pleasant nap. Bacon creates great depth of flavor, and dulse—which is sometimes called sea bacon—builds even more flavor. For a hearty weekday meal on a winter's day, warmed-up leftover gratin hits the spot.

SERVES 10

- 10 medium russet potatoes, peeled
- ¼ cup (72 g) plus 1 teaspoon kosher salt
- 8 slices thick-cut bacon, medium-diced
- 8 tablespoons (115 g/1 stick) unsalted butter
- 4 large leeks, white parts only, well rinsed and thinly sliced
- 4 garlic cloves, minced
- 1 cup (240 ml) dry white wine
- 1 quart (960 ml) heavy cream
- 2 tablespoons fresh thyme leaves
- 1 cup (90 g) grated Parmesan cheese
- ½ cup (40 g) panko bread crumbs
- ¼ cup (3 g) dulse flakes

1. In a soup pot, combine 4 quarts (3.84 L) water, the potatoes, and ¼ cup (72 g) of the salt and bring to a boil over high heat. Reduce the heat so the water maintains a low boil and cook the potatoes in the uncovered pot until they are fork-tender, 30 to 40 minutes.

2. Drain the cooked potatoes and set them aside to cool. When they are cool enough to handle, slice them into rounds ¼ inch (6 mm) thick.

3. Preheat the oven to 400°F (200°C).

4. While the potatoes are cooking and cooling, line a plate with paper towels and set it near the stove. Cook the bacon pieces in a large skillet over medium-low heat, stirring often, until crisp, 7 to 10 minutes. Remove the crisped bacon and set it aside on the paper towels. Pour out all but a slick of bacon fat from the pan. (You won't need the bacon fat to complete this recipe, so you can add it to your bacon fat jar—I hope you have one in your refrigerator. It's a guaranteed flavor picker-upper with pan-fried vegetables.)

5. Warm 6 tablespoons (85 g/¾ stick) of the butter in the same skillet over medium heat until it foams. Add the leeks, garlic, and remaining 1 teaspoon salt and cook, stirring frequently, until the vegetables are translucent, 5 to 7 minutes.

6. Add the white wine and deglaze the pan over high heat, scraping the bottom of the pan to get all the tasty bits. Reduce the liquid by half, about 3 minutes. Reduce the heat to medium-low and add the heavy cream, thyme, and bacon bits. Reduce the mixture until the cream coats the back of a spoon, about 8 minutes.

7. Meanwhile, use the remaining 2 tablespoons (30 g) butter to generously butter a 10-by-13-inch (25 by 33 cm) baking dish (or any casserole of similar capacity). Lay the potatoes in a single layer in the baking dish. Sprinkle with ½ cup (45 g) of the Parmesan. In a small bowl, combine the panko, dulse flakes, and remaining ½ cup (45 g) Parmesan.

8. Pour the cream mixture over the potatoes and top with the panko-Parmesan mixture. Transfer the baking dish to the oven and bake uncovered until the mixture thickens, bubbles on the edges, and turns brown on top, 12 to 15 minutes.

9. Let rest for 10 to 15 minutes before serving. Store any leftovers in an airtight container in the refrigerator for 3 to 4 days.

ASPARAGUS WITH GORGONZOLA SHALLOT BUTTER

Each spring, the sight of asparagus pushing up through dark soil signals the start of the annual parade of delicious vegetables. Oven-roasting asparagus with olive oil is the simplest of recipes. It explodes with flavor when you top it with this Gorgonzola shallot butter. It's sharp—but not too sharp—funky, creamy, and sweet. I especially like the contrast of the cold butter with the warm asparagus. You can use any type of blue cheese, but I am sentimental about Gorgonzola, which was the chef's blue cheese of choice in my first real restaurant job at the Lookout on the Blue Hill Peninsula. The butter is also terrific on a charcoal-grilled steak, roasted halibut, Brussels sprouts—my list could go on!

SERVES 4 AS AN APPETIZER

FOR THE GORGONZOLA SHALLOT BUTTER

- 8 tablespoons (115 g/1 stick) unsalted butter, at room temperature
- 3 ounces (82 g) crumbled Gorgonzola cheese
- 1 medium shallot, minced
- 2 tablespoons roughly chopped fresh flat-leaf parsley
- 1 teaspoon kosher salt

FOR THE ASPARAGUS

- 1 pound (455 g) asparagus
- 2 tablespoons grapeseed or canola oil

1. Preheat the oven to 400°F (200°C).

2. Make the Gorgonzola shallot butter: In a food processor or blender, combine the butter, Gorgonzola, shallot, parsley, and salt and pulse until the ingredients start to come together. Then process at a higher speed for 15 seconds. You're looking for a smooth, even distribution of the ingredients. Scrape down the sides as necessary. Transfer to a medium bowl and refrigerate for at least 30 minutes before serving. (The butter will keep for 5 days in the refrigerator and up to 3 months in the freezer.)

3. Meanwhile, cook the asparagus: Trim the asparagus, breaking off 1 to 2 inches (2.5 to 5 cm) from the tough bottoms. Rinse the asparagus thoroughly and dry on a clean kitchen towel. Transfer the asparagus to a baking sheet, drizzle on the oil, and roll the asparagus around in the oil to lightly coat. Transfer the baking sheet to the oven and roast for 10 minutes. Asparagus varies in thickness and people vary in how snappy they like their asparagus. Check the stalks every 5 minutes until they are done to your liking.

4. Transfer the cooked asparagus to a serving plate and top with cold Gorgonzola shallot butter. You be the judge about how buttery and cheesy you want the dish to be. I am from the school of "Too much ain't enough."

HONEYNUT HAND PIES AND SCORCHED RADICCHIO

Honeynut squash is one of the great new varieties of vegetables developed by Dan Barber and the Cornell College of Agriculture and Life Sciences. It was bred for deep sweet flavor and creamy texture. You can find it in many farmers' markets and frequently in supermarkets. Butternut squash will do fine as a substitute. The crispy crust of the hand pie and the contrast of the sweet squash and charred radicchio is really quite elegant. This is a great project to make with kids.

MAKES 8 HAND PIES

FOR THE ROUGH PUFF PASTRY DOUGH

2 cups (250 g) all-purpose flour, plus more for rolling

½ teaspoon kosher salt

8 ounces (225 g/2 sticks) cold unsalted butter

8 to 10 tablespoons (120 to 150 ml) cold water, as needed

FOR THE FILLING

2 to 3 honeynut squash (about 2½ pounds total) or 1 large butternut squash

1 medium shallot, thinly sliced

4 tablespoons (60 ml) olive oil

2 tablespoons maple syrup

3 teaspoons kosher salt

¼ teaspoon freshly ground black pepper

ingredients continue

1. Make the dough: In a large bowl, combine the flour and salt. Using a box grater, grate in the cold butter and mix by hand to incorporate it. Take care not to overwork the dough because you want the butter to remain in pea-size pieces. Add the cold water slowly and mix by hand until the dough barely comes together. It will be shaggy; no kneading needed. Cover the dough and let rest in the refrigerator for 30 minutes.

2. Dust a work surface with flour and roll out the dough into a rectangle, roughly 12 inches by 8 inches (30 by 20 cm). With a long side facing you, fold the right third over the center and then fold the left third over that, just as if you were folding a business letter. Rotate the dough 90 degrees, then roll it out and fold it again in the same manner. Cover the dough with a dry kitchen towel and refrigerate for 15 minutes. Repeat this process of rolling, folding, and chilling twice more.

3. Make the filling: Preheat the oven to 400°F (200°C). Line a baking sheet with parchment paper.

4. Peel the squash and cut it in half. Remove the seeds and strings and cut the squash into ¼-inch (6 mm) cubes. Place the squash and shallot in a large bowl and add 3 tablespoons of the olive oil, the maple syrup, 2 teaspoons of the salt, and the pepper; stir to combine. Spread the mixture in a single layer over the parchment-lined baking sheet and roast in the oven for 10 to

1 head radicchio, trimmed and sliced into 6 wedges

1 tablespoon minced fresh sage

Egg wash: 1 egg beaten with 1 tablespoon milk

12 minutes. Stir the mixture, rotate the baking sheet, and roast for about 10 minutes more, until the squash begins to brown and is tender and cooked through. Transfer the squash mixture back to the large bowl.

5. Warm a grill pan or skillet over high heat (or, if you are cooking outside, heat a charcoal or gas grill to high and use a grill basket over the grill). Drizzle the radicchio wedges with the remaining 1 tablespoon oil, season the wedges with the remaining 1 teaspoon salt, and cook the radicchio until it is charred and wilted, 3 to 5 minutes. Remove the radicchio from the pan to a cutting board and roughly chop. Add the radicchio and the sage to the bowl with the squash mixture and gently stir. Check the seasoning and adjust as necessary. Set the vegetables aside to cool before assembling the pies.

6. When you are ready to proceed, preheat the oven to 375°F (190°C). Line a baking sheet with parchment paper.

7. On a floured work surface, roll out the dough until it is very thin, about ⅛ inch (3 mm) thick. Using a bowl or small plate as a guide, cut the dough into eight 6-inch (15 cm) circles. Place ¼ cup (60 g) of the vegetable mixture on the left half of each dough round, leaving a ½-inch (13 mm) border on the outer rim. Brush the outer edges of the dough with the egg wash. Fold the right half over and press the edges together with your fingers, then seal the hand pie using the tines of a fork. Transfer the pies to the lined baking sheet. If you have enough dough trimmings left over, you can reroll them for an additional pie. Brush the tops of the pies with the remaining egg wash. Using a paring knife, cut two or three small slits in the top of each pie to allow steam to vent. This prevents the pies from cracking open during baking.

8. Bake until golden brown, 30 to 35 minutes. Remove the pies from the baking sheet and set them aside on a wire rack until they are cool enough to handle, about 10 minutes. As you might guess from the name of this recipe, you can eat them with your hands. The pies are best eaten the day they're made but will keep, tightly wrapped, in the refrigerator for up to 2 days.

ROASTED DELICATA SQUASH WITH APPLE CIDER GLAZE

When delicata squash shows up in the market, I'm ready to start settling into autumn mode: cooler nights, the first fires in the woodstove, and a light sweater in the morning. Delicata is a kind of midway point between summer squash and the butternut and acorn squash to come. It has a bit of sweet potato denseness, a skin that is a little chewy and a little crisp, and seeds that are nutty and crunchy. Here, it's glazed with fresh-pressed apple cider reduced to syrupy deliciousness—a fall treat in my kitchen.

SERVES 4

FOR THE SQUASH

2 delicata squash, sliced into ½-inch-thick (13 mm) rounds (leave the seeds intact)

2 tablespoons minced fresh flat-leaf parsley leaves, plus more for garnish

1 tablespoon chopped fresh lemon thyme, plus more for garnish

1 tablespoon kosher salt

2 tablespoons olive oil

2 tablespoons (30 g) unsalted butter

FOR THE APPLE CIDER GLAZE

½ teaspoon mustard seeds

¼ teaspoon fennel seeds

2 cups (480 ml) apple cider

¼ teaspoon kosher salt

1. Prepare the squash: Preheat the oven to 400°F (200°C).

2. In a large bowl, toss together the squash, parsley, lemon thyme, and salt. Pour in the olive oil and toss again. Spread the squash out on a baking sheet and scatter bits of the butter over the squash. Transfer to the oven and roast until lightly browned on the bottom and cooked through, 30 minutes.

3. Meanwhile, make the apple cider glaze: Toast the mustard seeds and fennel seeds in a dry nonreactive 2-quart (1.92 L) saucepan over medium heat, swirling the pan and taking care not to burn the seeds. Just as soon as you smell the seeds' aroma, about 1 minute, add the apple cider and salt. Cook until the mixture reduces enough to coat the back of a spoon and becomes syrupy, about 30 minutes. Keep an eye on it, stirring from time to time, so that it doesn't stick to the pan. As it reduces, the glaze will bubble up, so reduce the heat under the pan as needed. Pour the glaze into a smaller saucepan for rewarming later. At this point, there should be roughly 2 tablespoons of glaze.

4. To serve, place the roasted delicata squash on a platter, pour the cider glaze over the top, and garnish with parsley and thyme. Store any leftovers in an airtight container in the refrigerator for up to 3 days.

CREAM SOUPS FOR ALL SEASONS

Cream soups are rich in flavor and pamper your palate with their smooth texture. These four soups are an especially delicious way to showcase the subtle elegance of Roasted Vegetable Stock (page 302), a purely vegetable-based stock that carries layers of flavor and the ripe tastes of the garden. The method for the four seasonal cream soups is basically the same—the differences reflect the featured vegetables and garnishes. Once you get the hang of the method, feel free to try the soups with other vegetables in the leading role.

SPRING GREEN PEA CREAM SOUP

SERVES 4

8 tablespoons (115 g/1 stick) unsalted butter

1 medium shallot, finely diced

1 medium leek, well rinsed and thinly sliced

1 medium russet potato (about 8 ounces/225 g), peeled and roughly chopped

½ teaspoon kosher salt, plus more to taste

1 cup (500 g) green peas (fresh or thawed frozen)

2 garlic cloves, minced

3 cups (720 ml) Roasted Vegetable Stock (page 302)

2 bay leaves

1 cup (240 ml) heavy cream

2 cups (60 g) spinach

½ cup (25 g) fresh dill, plus more for garnish

¼ cup (13 g) fresh mint leaves, plus more for garnish

1 teaspoon sherry vinegar

1. In a soup pot or Dutch oven, warm the butter over medium heat until it foams. Add the shallot, leek, potato, and salt and cook for 5 minutes, stirring from time to time so that the vegetables soften but do not brown. Add the peas and garlic and cook until the peas soften, 5 minutes. Add the stock and bay leaves to the pot and bring the liquid to a medium simmer. Cook until the potatoes are tender, 20 minutes. Add the heavy cream and simmer for another 5 minutes, stirring from time to time.

2. Remove the pot from the heat and discard the bay leaves. Working in batches, transfer the contents of the pot, along with the spinach, dill, and mint, to a blender or food processor and puree until smooth. Add the vinegar and pulse. Pass the soup through a fine-mesh strainer to remove the vegetable fiber. Season with salt to taste.

3. Serve warm in bowls or mugs, garnished with dill and mint. Leftovers will keep in an airtight container in the refrigerator for up to 3 days.

SUMMER RED PEPPER CREAM SOUP

SERVES 4

8 tablespoons (115 g/1 stick) unsalted butter

4 red bell peppers, roughly chopped

1 medium shallot, finely diced

1 medium leek, well rinsed and thinly sliced

1 medium russet potato (about 8 ounces/225 g), peeled and roughly chopped

½ teaspoon kosher salt, plus more to taste

2 garlic cloves, minced

Leaves from 4 thyme sprigs

3 cups (720 ml) Roasted Vegetable Stock (page 302)

2 bay leaves

1 cup (240 ml) heavy cream

1 teaspoon sherry vinegar

Fresh dill, mint, or other herbs, for garnish

1. In a soup pot or Dutch oven, warm the butter over medium heat until it foams. Add the peppers, shallot, leek, potato, and salt and cook for 5 minutes, stirring from time to time so that the vegetables soften but do not brown. Add the garlic and thyme and cook until the vegetables soften further, 5 minutes. Add the stock and bay leaves and bring the liquid to a medium simmer. Cook until the potatoes are tender, 20 minutes. Add the heavy cream and simmer for another 5 minutes, stirring from time to time.

2. Remove the pot from the heat and discard the bay leaves. Working in batches, transfer the contents of the pot to a blender or food processor and puree until smooth. Add the vinegar and pulse. Pass the soup through a fine-mesh strainer to remove the vegetable fiber. Season with salt to taste.

3. Serve warm or chilled in bowls or mugs, garnished with dill, mint, or your herb of choice. Leftovers will keep in an airtight container in the refrigerator for up to 3 days.

AUTUMN HONEYNUT SQUASH AND APPLE CIDER CREAM SOUP

SERVES 4

8 tablespoons (115 g/1 stick) unsalted butter

2 small honeynut squash, peeled, seeded, and chopped

2 green apples, peeled, cored, and chopped

1 medium shallot, finely diced

1 medium leek, well rinsed and thinly sliced

Leaves from 4 thyme sprigs

½ teaspoon kosher salt, plus more to taste

2 cups (480 ml) Roasted Vegetable Stock (page 302)

1 cup (240 ml) apple cider

2 bay leaves

1 cup (240 ml) heavy cream

1 teaspoon apple cider vinegar

Fresh parsley leaves or dill, for garnish

1. In a soup pot or Dutch oven, warm the butter over medium heat until it foams. Add the squash, apple, shallot, leek, thyme, and salt and cook for 10 minutes, stirring from time to time so that the vegetables soften but do not brown. Add the stock, apple cider, and bay leaves and bring the liquid to a medium simmer. Cook for 20 minutes, until the squash is tender. Add the heavy cream and simmer for another 5 minutes, stirring from time to time.

2. Remove the pot from the heat and discard the bay leaves. Working in batches, transfer the contents of the pot to a blender or food processor and puree until smooth. Add the vinegar and pulse. Pass the soup through a fine-mesh strainer to remove the vegetable fiber. Season with salt to taste.

3. Serve warm in bowls or mugs, garnished with parsley or dill. Leftovers will keep in an airtight container in the refrigerator for up to 3 days.

WINTER CELERY CREAM SOUP

SERVES 4

- 8 tablespoons (115 g/1 stick) unsalted butter
- 1 pound celery (about 1 bunch), roughly chopped
- 1 medium shallot, finely diced
- 1 medium leek, well rinsed and thinly sliced
- 1 medium russet potato (about 8 ounces/225 g), peeled and roughly chopped
- ½ teaspoon kosher salt, plus more to taste
- 3 cups (720 ml) Roasted Vegetable Stock (page 302)
- 2 bay leaves
- 1 cup (240 ml) heavy cream
- 2 cups (60 g) spinach
- ½ cup (25 g) fresh dill, plus more for garnish
- 1 teaspoon sherry vinegar

1. In a soup pot or Dutch oven, warm the butter over medium heat until it foams. Add the celery, shallot, leek, potato, and salt and cook for 10 minutes, stirring from time to time so that the vegetables soften but do not brown. Add the stock and bay leaves and bring the liquid to a medium simmer. Cook for 20 minutes, until the potatoes are tender. Add the heavy cream and simmer for another 5 minutes, stirring from time to time.

2. Remove the pot from the heat and discard the bay leaves. Working in batches, transfer the contents of the pot, along with the spinach and dill, to a blender or food processor and puree until smooth. Add the vinegar and pulse. Pass the soup through a fine-mesh strainer to remove the vegetable fiber. Season with salt to taste.

3. Serve warm or chilled in bowls or mugs, garnished with the dill. Leftovers will keep in an airtight container in the refrigerator for up to 3 days.

VARIATION

For a vegan version of these soups, simply omit the cream and add an extra cup of vegetable stock. The garden flavors will come through perfectly.

PAN-ROASTED BRUSSELS SPROUT KIMCHI

Sometimes just a few ingredients can produce the most powerful flavors and pleasing textures. For this side dish, I make my own kimchi, but it is readily available in Asian markets and many supermarkets. Think of it as amped-up sauerkraut that gives an umami punch to Brussels sprouts. Serve this dish alongside Venison Tenderloin (page 198), deep-fried seafood, or Stuffed Double-Cut Pork Chops in place of the cabbage mix (page 186).

SERVES 4

1 pound (455 g) Brussels sprouts

1 cup (150 g) kimchi

¼ cup (60 ml) toasted sesame oil

½ to 1 teaspoon kosher salt, plus more as needed

1. Preheat the oven to 425°F (220°C).

2. Halve the Brussels sprouts lengthwise and discard the wilted outer leaves. Transfer the sprouts to a large bowl. Roughly chop the kimchi and add it to the bowl with the Brussels sprouts. Add the sesame oil and salt and toss to coat. Spread the mixture out evenly on a baking sheet (you want the mixture to cook evenly, so don't crowd the baking sheet) and roast for 10 minutes, then give it all a mix with a spatula. Roast for another 10 minutes, or until the Brussels sprouts brown or caramelize on the edges. The Brussels sprouts may develop a bit of char, which adds nicely to the flavor of this dish. Serve on a platter with a little more salt sprinkled over the top, if desired.

BEET RISOTTO

In one of my early jobs as a chef, in the town of Blue Hill, just north of Deer Isle, I wanted to create a vibrant version of risotto. The addition of pureed beets lent rich color, sweetness, and a velvety texture to a traditional risotto. This dish is now a standby in my home kitchen in the winter, when there aren't any fresh vegetables to pick. Butternut squash and pumpkin would also work well in this preparation, which includes a finish of horseradish cream sauce.

SERVES 4

FOR THE BEET RISOTTO

12 ounces (340 g) assorted-color beets, well scrubbed

4 tablespoons (60 ml) extra-virgin olive oil

Kosher salt

1 teaspoon sherry vinegar

Freshly ground black pepper

3 cups (720 ml) vegetable stock, homemade (page 302) or store-bought

1 large shallot, finely diced

2 garlic cloves, minced

1 tablespoon fresh thyme

1 cup (200 g) Arborio rice

½ cup (120 ml) dry white wine

½ cup (50 g) grated Parmesan cheese

FOR THE HORSERADISH CREAM

1 cup (250 g) crème fraîche or sour cream

1 tablespoon prepared horseradish

1. Make the beet risotto: Preheat the oven to 375°F (190°C).

2. Peel and very thinly slice one light-colored beet on a mandolin and set aside in a small bowl. Place the remaining beets on separate pieces of aluminum foil according to color. Drizzle the beets with 2 tablespoons of the oil and sprinkle salt over each beet. Tightly wrap the beets in the foil and bake until fork-tender, about 40 minutes. Remove the beets from the oven and let them rest for 10 minutes. Using paper towels or a dish rag, rub the skin off the warm beets and then roughly dice them. Reserve about 1 cup (250 g) of diced purple beets for the puree. Place the rest of the diced beets in a large bowl, toss with the vinegar, season with salt and pepper, and set aside. Combine the reserved purple beets with 1 cup (240 ml) of the stock in a blender or food processor and puree. Set the puree aside.

3. Bring the remaining 2 cups (480 ml) stock to a simmer in a 2-quart (1.92 L) saucepan. In a separate 4-quart (3.84 L) saucepan, warm the remaining 2 tablespoons oil over medium heat until it shimmers. Add the shallot to the pan with the oil and cook until translucent, about 2 minutes. Add the garlic and thyme and cook for another minute. Add the rice and stir thoroughly. Add the white wine and stir. Add the reserved beet puree and stir. Add a ladle of stock and stir until it is nearly absorbed, continuing to add additional stock, one ladle at a time and stirring, until the rice is cooked al dente. This should take about 20 minutes. Taste a grain of rice from time to time. Some rice absorbs liquid more slowly, so you may need to add up to 1 cup (240 ml) hot water to the

Kosher salt and freshly ground black pepper

FOR SERVING

2 teaspoons grated orange zest

2 teaspoons fresh dill

stock. After the rice is cooked, remove from the heat and stir in the Parmesan and ½ teaspoon salt. Adjust the seasonings to taste.

4. Make the horseradish cream: In a small bowl, whisk together the crème fraîche and horseradish and season to taste with salt and pepper.

5. To serve: Place a serving of the risotto in the middle of a wide soup plate. Top with a few dollops of horseradish cream, garnish with the reserved beet slices, and finish with a scattering of orange zest and dill. Store any leftovers in an airtight container in the refrigerator for up to 4 days.

BEAN-HOLE BAKED BEANS

In the days of the great lumber camps in Maine's northern forests, camp cooks would dig a hole and build a fire in it, and when the fire had burned down to coals, they'd set a Dutch oven filled with beans, salt pork, molasses, water, and other flavoring ingredients into the hole. Once the pot was well snuggled into the embers, they'd fill the hole back up and leave the beans to cook for 5 or 6 hours. Though I often make this recipe in a pit on the beach, it'll come out just as good if you make it in your home oven. For my changeup on the old-time lumberjack's recipe, I add a few cups of freshly pressed apple cider to the pot. These beans go as a side dish with pretty much anything. Put a fried egg on top and it's a meal.

SERVES 10

- 2 cups (400 g) dried Marfax beans or yellow-eyed peas (see Notes), rinsed, picked over for debris, and soaked overnight
- 2 cups (480 ml) apple cider
- 8 ounces (225 g) salt pork, roughly diced
- 2 large onions, medium-diced
- 2 tablespoons roughly chopped garlic
- 3 bay leaves or foraged winter bay
- ¼ cup (60 ml) molasses
- 3 tablespoons mustard powder
- 2 tablespoons freshly ground black pepper
- Grated zest and juice of 1 lemon
- 2 tablespoons kosher salt

ingredients continue

1. Position a rack in the bottom third of the oven and preheat the oven to 325°F (160°C).

2. In a nonreactive Dutch oven, combine the beans with 1 quart (960 ml) water and the apple cider. Bring to a boil over medium-high heat and cook the beans for 15 minutes. Turn off the heat and add the salt pork, onions, garlic, bay leaves, molasses, mustard powder, pepper, lemon zest, and lemon juice. Stir a few times. Place the lid on the Dutch oven and transfer to the oven.

3. Cook for 1 hour and then check that the beans are still covered by about 1 inch (2.5 cm) of liquid; add more water as necessary. Stir in the salt, cover, and continue to cook until the beans are soft and creamy, perhaps another 1 to 2 hours (or more) depending on the freshness of the beans (see Notes). Taste for doneness from time to time, making sure that the beans remain covered by about 1 inch (2.5 cm) of liquid. At this point, if the beans are nicely soft on the inside but the skins are still tough, add the baking soda. The beans will briefly foam as the baking soda reacts with the beans and their liquid. Cover the beans and cook for another 5 minutes and they should be ready to serve. Store leftovers in an airtight container in the refrigerator for up to 4 days.

recipe continues

¼ teaspoon baking soda (optional)

NOTES: Marfax beans grow well in Maine's cool climate, as do yellow-eyed peas. We use them whenever we make baked beans, but if all you have are navy beans or cannellini beans, they do equally well with this recipe.

Cooking time for beans will vary tremendously depending on how fresh they are. Really fresh beans can be soft and creamy in under 2 hours. Beans that have been stored a while will take longer. If you get to a point in the cooking where the beans are soft inside but still have tough skins, adding a little bit of baking soda to the pot often helps soften the skins.

SEEDED CRACKERS AND RED WINE APPLE BUTTER

These delicate, nutty-tasting crackers are gluten-free and vegan. They're quite lovely served with pâté, smoked fish, or cheese. I always have a cookie jar of them on my kitchen counter at home. When I'm hankering for a nosh, I slather some red wine apple butter on a few seeded crackers and it hits the spot.

MAKES 1 BAKING SHEET'S WORTH OF CRACKERS

½ cup (75 g) white sesame seeds

½ cup (75 g) black sesame seeds

½ cup (75 g) millet

½ cup (75 g) flax meal

½ cup (75 g) raw pumpkin seeds

⅓ cup (60 g) corn flour

2 teaspoons kosher salt

¼ cup (60 ml) canola or grapeseed oil

1 cup (240 ml) boiling water

Red Wine Apple Butter (recipe follows), for serving

Soft cheese, such as Brillat-Savarin, for serving (optional)

1. In a medium bowl, combine the white and black sesame seeds, millet, flax meal, pumpkin seeds, corn flour, and salt. Stir in the oil and then add the boiling water carefully to avoid spatter. Mix well to combine. Cover the bowl with plastic wrap and let rest for 30 minutes.

2. Preheat the oven to 350°F (180°C). Line a rimmed baking sheet with parchment paper.

3. Transfer the mixture from the bowl to the center of the prepared baking sheet. Place another piece of parchment over the mixture and, using a rolling pin, flatten it into a thin layer, about ¼ inch (6 mm) thick.

4. Remove the top sheet of parchment. Bake for about 40 minutes, until dry and golden brown. Remove the baking sheet from the oven and set it aside to cool for 30 minutes, then break the crackers into irregular-sized pieces.

5. Serve the crackers with apple butter or with a soft cheese, if desired. They will keep in an airtight container at room temperature for up to 2 weeks.

Red Wine Apple Butter

MAKES 6 CUPS (ABOUT 1.4 L)

- 12 Honeycrisp apples or any sweet red apple, cored and roughly chopped
- 2 cups (480 ml) red wine (any kind is fine)
- 1¼ cups packed (275 g) dark brown sugar

When it's apple-picking time, we have apples in great abundance, and this gorgeous burgundy-red apple butter is a great way to use a lot of them (while still leaving some apples on the ground for our wildlife). It's important that you use apples with red skins to deepen the color from the red wine. I've served this on seared duck breast and roast pork chops, with foie gras, and on a cheese board. Keep some on hand and you're sure to come up with new uses on your own.

1. Place the apples in a Dutch oven or large pot. Add the red wine and brown sugar and cook over medium-low heat, stirring well from time to time, until the apples are soft and tender, 10 to 15 minutes.

2. Transfer the apples to a blender or food processor and blend at medium speed for 1 minute. Return the mixture to the pot and cook over low heat until the mixture thickens and becomes slightly sticky, 5 to 10 minutes. Remove from the heat.

3. If serving with crackers, transfer the apple butter from the pot to a serving bowl and, once it has cooled somewhat, serve. Otherwise, let cool and store in an airtight container in the refrigerator for 5 to 7 days.

GNOCCHI WITH WILD MUSHROOM SAUCE

Gnocchi are a holy matrimony of potatoes, flour, and eggs. Potatoes give them creaminess and the flour-and-egg mixture creates the pasta-like texture. Rolling out the mixture into logs and trimming them to bite-size is a nice exercise in being in the moment for a pleasantly repetitive task. In Italy, people say perfect gnocchi should be the size of a small child's thumb. If you have small children, definitely invite them to help in the gnocchi-making. Gnocchi are classically served with sage and brown butter, but here you'll pair them with a sauce of wild mushrooms.

SERVES 4 TO 6

FOR THE DOUGH

1½ pounds (680 g) russet potatoes

Kosher salt

1 cup (125 g) all-purpose flour, plus more for dusting

1 large egg

4 egg yolks

2 tablespoons (30 g) unsalted butter

2 tablespoons olive oil, plus more as needed

FOR THE WILD MUSHROOM SAUCE

2 tablespoons (30 g) unsalted butter

1 medium shallot, finely diced

3 garlic cloves, minced

2 tablespoons olive oil, plus more as needed

ingredients continue

1. Make the dough: Preheat the oven to 375°F (190°C).

2. Bake the potatoes on a baking sheet until soft, about 1 hour 15 minutes.

3. Set the potatoes aside until cool enough to handle. Scoop out the potato flesh and discard the skins. Using a potato ricer or food mill, rice the potatoes into a bowl and season with ½ teaspoon kosher salt.

4. Add the flour, whole egg, and egg yolks to the riced potatoes. Gently mix until the combination forms a dough. Knead lightly until the dough holds together. Turn the dough out of the bowl onto a clean work surface, cover, and let rest for 15 minutes.

5. Bring a soup pot filled halfway with liberally salted water to a boil over high heat.

6. Dust a work surface with flour and roll the dough into a thick log (see photos, page 259). Using a pastry cutter, bench scraper, or knife, divide the log into 4 equal portions. Dust the work surface again and roll the first portion into a rope ½ to ¾ inch (1.3 to 2 cm) thick. Cut the rope into roughly 1-inch (2.5 cm) lengths. Repeat with the rest of the dough.

7. To create ridges on the gnocchi, if desired, dust your hands with flour as needed and, pressing very lightly, roll the gnocchi

- 1 pound (455 g) any mix of oyster mushrooms, maitakes, chanterelles, or shiitakes, cleaned and trimmed
- 1½ cups (360 ml) heavy cream
- ½ cup (50 g) grated Parmesan cheese
- ¼ cup (13 g) chopped fresh flat-leaf parsley
- ½ teaspoon kosher salt
- ½ teaspoon freshly ground black pepper

along the back of a fork. If you make gnocchi frequently, a notched gnocchi board (see Notes and photo, opposite) is inexpensive and practical.

8. Remove the raw gnocchi to a baking sheet lightly dusted with flour. If you want to freeze the gnocchi to enjoy later, you can make them up to this point (see Notes).

9. Working in batches, boil the gnocchi until they float, about 3 minutes. Using a slotted spoon, remove the cooked gnocchi to a bowl and toss them in some olive oil. Use enough oil that the gnocchi don't stick to each other.

10. In a 12-inch (30 cm) skillet, combine the butter and 2 tablespoons olive oil and heat over medium-high heat until the butter melts and starts to foam. Working in batches to avoid overcrowding, add the gnocchi to the skillet and cook over medium heat until they are nicely browned and crisped, about 1 minute per side. Remove the gnocchi to a bowl and set aside.

11. Make the wild mushroom sauce: In the same skillet you used to cook the gnocchi, warm 1 tablespoon (15 g) of the butter over medium heat until it foams. Add the shallot and garlic and cook for 1 minute. Add the remaining 1 tablespoon (15 g) butter and the olive oil and heat until the butter starts to foam. Add the mushrooms and toss to coat with the butter and oil. You may need a little bit more oil. Cook the mushrooms until they soften, 5 to 7 minutes.

12. Add the heavy cream and let it thicken over medium heat for 3 to 5 minutes. Add the gnocchi to the skillet and toss the mixture to coat. Add the Parmesan, parsley, salt, and pepper, stir to combine, and serve. Store leftovers in an airtight container in the refrigerator for up to 3 days.

NOTES: Williams Sonoma makes a nice gnocchi board that comes with a dowel for easier rolling.

You can prepare the gnocchi in advance and store in the freezer for up to 2 months. Cook them directly from frozen.

DESSERTS

When friends invite me to a potluck, I will often be the one to sign up for dessert. To me, making dessert means a quieter time in the kitchen, when shafts of late-afternoon sun pour through the windows and the house fills with the scent of something sweet in the oven. Baking especially is a process of waiting. It can't be hurried, and that is a blessing in our hurry-up world.

Another plus for volunteering to make dessert: You are pretty much guaranteed to please most people. I mean, who doesn't like dessert? People can get finicky about fishes, or have a problem with meat, but everyone loves sweetness, and crunch, and creaminess. Dessert is an homage to the first taste that we humans enjoy. It runs like a melody all through life.

Like pretty much everyone in Maine, I treasure the season when each fruit is in its glorious moment: Strawberries to make strawberry shortcake (see page 265), then blueberries for a pavlova (see page 287), and peaches, apples, and pears each take a turn. Whether it's pies, cakes, tarts, or purees, there's always a way to top off a meal with fruit. There's also a time of year—winter and early spring—when pantry items (flour, nuts, sugar, syrup, and chocolate) can be combined in endless variations of taste and texture.

STRAWBERRY SHORTCAKE WITH MAPLE-LAVENDER WHIPPED CREAM

Briefly cooking strawberries in a hot skillet concentrates their sweetness and produces delicious ruby-red juices that get sopped up by the shortcake biscuit. The maple-lavender flavor in the whipped cream is inspired by the cuisine of Provence in the south of France, where the combination of lavender and honey is widely used. For my Deer Isle version, I infuse the cream with pesticide-free lavender petals from my garden and sweeten it with maple syrup. The best way to serve this dessert is to put out a tray with the shortcake biscuits, a bowl with the strawberries, and another bowl with the whipped cream and let your guests assemble their own dessert.

MAKES 8 SHORTCAKES

FOR THE LAVENDER CREAM

1½ cups (360 ml) heavy cream

1 tablespoon dried culinary lavender

FOR THE SHORTCAKES

2¾ cups (345 g) all-purpose flour, plus more for dusting

⅓ cup (65 g) sugar

2 teaspoons baking powder

1 teaspoon kosher salt

¼ teaspoon baking soda

6 ounces (170 g/1½ sticks) cold unsalted butter, cubed

2 large eggs

½ cup (120 ml) heavy cream, plus more for brushing

ingredients continue

1. Make the lavender cream: In a small saucepan, combine the heavy cream and lavender and bring to a simmer over medium-low heat, stirring often. As soon as it reaches a simmer, remove from the heat and pour the mixture into a small heatproof bowl or jug. Let cool for 15 minutes, then refrigerate until completely cooled, about 2 hours.

2. Make the shortcakes: In a stand mixer fitted with the paddle, combine the flour, sugar, baking powder, salt, and baking soda. Beat the mixture at medium speed until it is evenly combined, about 20 seconds. Add the butter and beat on low speed until the butter is broken into crumbly pea-size pieces, 1 to 2 minutes.

3. In a small bowl, whisk together the eggs, plain heavy cream, lemon zest, and lemon juice. Add the egg mixture to the flour mixture in the stand mixer, beating on low speed until the mixture is evenly moistened, about 15 seconds.

4. Line a rimmed baking sheet with parchment paper. Turn the dough out onto a floured work surface and knead once or twice, until the dough just comes together. Dust the top of the dough with flour and roll it out to a 1-inch (2.5 cm) thickness. Using a

1 tablespoon grated lemon zest

1 tablespoon fresh lemon juice

FOR THE STRAWBERRIES

1 quart (about 600 g) strawberries, rinsed, hulled, and halved

3 tablespoons sugar

Juice of 1 lemon

FOR THE WHIPPED CREAM

2 tablespoons maple syrup

Dash of kosher salt

lightly floured 3-inch (7.5 cm) cookie cutter, cut the dough into rounds and transfer them to the lined baking sheet. Gather and reroll the scraps and cut out more rounds so that you end up with 8. Transfer the shortcake rounds to the freezer and chill for 5 to 10 minutes to firm them up.

5. Preheat the oven to 400°F (200°C).

6. Remove the shortcake rounds from the freezer and brush them with some heavy cream. Transfer to the oven and bake for 15 minutes, or until the biscuits are lightly golden. Transfer to a wire rack to cool.

7. Prepare the strawberries: Place a large cast-iron skillet over medium-high heat for a few minutes until the skillet is quite hot. In a medium bowl, stir together the strawberries and sugar. Add the mixture to the skillet and cook until the berries are slightly softened and release some of their juices, about 2 minutes. Return the strawberries and their juices to the medium bowl and stir in the lemon juice.

8. Make the whipped cream: Remove the lavender cream from the refrigerator and strain through a fine-mesh sieve into a large bowl. Discard the lavender. Stir in the maple syrup and salt and whisk vigorously until medium stiff peaks form.

9. To assemble, split the shortcakes in half horizontally. Spoon 2 to 3 tablespoonfuls of strawberries over the bottom half of each shortcake. Add a large dollop of maple-lavender whipped cream over the strawberries and place the other half of the shortcake on top.

ROBIOLA CHEESECAKE WITH CHARRED STRAWBERRY SAUCE

Basque cheesecakes were invented in the 1990s by Santiago Rivera in his restaurant, La Viña, in San Sebastián, Spain. He was looking to make a cheesecake without a crust. He made his with a cream cheese that's pretty similar to Philadelphia cream cheese. In addition to cream cheese, I make mine with fresh Robiola—an Italian cheese with just a teeny tad of funk that gives it an elegant finish. Fresh strawberries are in season in Maine in June and July. I steep them in vermouth to make a sweet, slightly bitter, fruity sauce that balances the creaminess of the cheese. Baking at a high temperature produces a seductive dark crust—the rich brown color of an old violin. Charred strawberries are a rustic finishing touch.

MAKES ONE 9-INCH (23 CM) CAKE

- Softened butter, for the parchment paper
- 1 quart (about 600 g) strawberries, rinsed, hulled, and halved
- 2 cups (480 ml) sweet vermouth
- 10 ounces (285 g) cream cheese
- 10 ounces (285 g) fresh Robiola cheese
- ¾ cup (150 g) plus 2 tablespoons granulated sugar
- ½ cup (120 ml) heavy cream
- 2 large eggs
- 2 tablespoons (30 g) cold unsalted butter
- 2 tablespoons powdered sugar

1. Preheat the oven to 450°F (230°C). Line a 9-inch (23 cm) springform pan with two crisscrossed pieces of buttered parchment paper, making sure that the parchment extends about 2 inches (5 cm) above the rim of the springform pan. This will make it easier to release the cake after baking.

2. Set aside ½ cup (150 g) strawberries for charring. Place the remaining strawberries in a bowl. Add the vermouth to cover the berries and refrigerate for at least 2 hours. To char the reserved strawberries, heat a cast-iron skillet or ridged grill pan over high heat. When the pan is hot, place the strawberries in the pan and heat for 1 to 2 minutes, until they begin to char. Remove the berries to a small bowl and set aside.

3. In a stand mixer fitted with the paddle, combine the cream cheese, Robiola, ¾ cup (150 g) of the granulated sugar, the heavy cream, and eggs. Mix on medium speed until the ingredients are uniformly combined, 8 to 10 minutes.

4. Fill the lined springform pan with the cream cheese mixture. Place the springform pan on a baking sheet and transfer to the oven.

recipe continues

5. Bake for 25 minutes. Look for the top of the cake to turn dark brown. If it's not brown yet, give it a few more minutes in the oven, then remove the cake from the oven. The cheesecake should jiggle a little, but it will firm up as it cools and sink a bit in the center.

6. Set the cheesecake on a wire rack to cool. When it has cooled to room temperature, gently remove the springform sides and the parchment paper. You can also leave the cake in the springform pan and refrigerate for 2 hours if you like a chilled cheesecake.

7. When almost ready to serve, remove the strawberries and vermouth from the refrigerator. Using a slotted spoon, transfer ½ cup (75 g) of the strawberries to a small bowl and set aside.

8. In a deep saucepan, combine the strawberries and vermouth with the remaining 2 tablespoons granulated sugar. Cook over medium-high heat until the mixture is sticky and syrupy, about 8 minutes. Remove the saucepan from the heat and stir in the cold butter.

9. Pour the sauce over the cake and decorate with the reserved charred strawberries. Sprinkle with the powdered sugar and slice to serve. Store the cake in the refrigerator for up to 3 days.

PEACH RASPBERRY UPSIDE-DOWN CAKE

When I was in second grade, we cooked our way through the alphabet, so for the letter "A," one of my classmates picked "apple" and made applesauce (with help from our teacher). Another kid picked "B" and baked bread. I claimed the letter "P" because I really loved pineapple upside-down cake. In this recipe I use two of my favorite summer fruits, peaches and raspberries, to make a seasonal upside-down cake. The one quality that all successful upside-down cake makers have in common can be summed up in a single word: faith. With faith, your upside-down cake will unmold when you turn it right side up. When you prepare the cake, the fruit will be on the bottom, but when the cake is turned upside down and unmolded, the fruit will end up on top.

MAKES ONE 9-INCH (23 CM) CAKE

Softened butter, for the pan
Light brown sugar, for the pan

FOR THE FRUIT LAYER

8 tablespoons (115 g/1 stick) unsalted butter, at room temperature
1 cup loosely packed (220 g) light brown sugar
2 tablespoons maple syrup
1 teaspoon rum
¼ teaspoon vanilla extract
Pinch of kosher salt
2 large peaches, pitted and cut into ½-inch (13 mm) slices
1½ cups (190 g) raspberries

1. Preheat the oven to 350°F (180°C). Prepare a 9-inch (23 cm) round cake pan with a light coating of butter and a sprinkling of brown sugar.

2. Prepare the fruit layer: In a stand mixer fitted with the paddle (or in a large bowl with a hand mixer), combine the butter, brown sugar, maple syrup, rum, vanilla, and salt and beat at medium speed until smooth and well blended, 8 to 10 minutes.

3. Spread the mixture over the bottom of the cake pan. Arrange the sliced peaches and raspberries on top of this layer, starting with a ring of peaches, then a ring of raspberries, and filling the center area with overlapping peach slices.

4. Make the batter: In a stand mixer fitted with the paddle, combine the butter, granulated sugar, brown sugar, and vanilla and beat on low speed until creamy, about 3 minutes, scraping down the sides of the bowl as needed. Beat in the eggs, one at a time. Add the crème fraîche and milk, continuing to beat on low.

5. In a small bowl, sift the flour and baking powder together. Slowly add this mixture to the stand mixer and beat until incorporated into a smooth batter, 2 to 3 minutes.

FOR THE BATTER

8 tablespoons (115 g/1 stick) unsalted butter, at room temperature

⅓ cup (65 g) granulated sugar

⅓ cup loosely packed (75 g) light brown sugar

½ teaspoon vanilla extract

2 large eggs

2 tablespoons crème fraîche

2 tablespoons milk

1¼ cups (155 g) all-purpose flour

2 teaspoons baking powder

FOR THE TOPPING

⅓ cup loosely packed (75 g) light brown sugar

1 large peach, roughly chopped

1 cup (240 ml) crème fraîche or sour cream

½ cup (60 g) raspberries

1 tablespoon chopped fresh mint

6. Spoon the batter into the prepared cake pan, smoothing with a spatula. Place the cake pan on a baking sheet and transfer to the oven.

7. Bake for 15 minutes. Rotate the pan front to back and bake 25 minutes more, or until a cake tester comes out clean and the cake is lightly golden around the edges.

8. Let the cake cool in the pan on a wire rack for 25 minutes.

9. Prepare the topping: In a large skillet, combine the brown sugar and 1 tablespoon water and warm over medium heat until the sugar dissolves. Add the chopped peaches and cook until they are a smooth uniform mixture, about 3 minutes. Transfer the mixture to a food processor or blender. Blend, starting at a slower speed so as not to spatter and then increasing the speed, until completely smooth.

10. In a medium bowl, whisk the crème fraîche by hand until it is fluffy. Using a rubber spatula, fold the peach puree into the whipped crème fraîche.

11. To release the cake from the pan, run a knife around the edges and carefully invert it onto a plate (see photo, page 272). To serve, spoon the puree onto a dessert plate, place a slice of cake on top of the puree, and top the cake with the raspberries and fresh mint.

12. Store the cake in the refrigerator for up to 5 days, without the crème fraîche and fruit topping. If you store it with the topping on, eat the cake within 3 days.

WHOOPIE PIES

There has been a long feud between Maine and Pennsylvania about where the whoopie pie was invented. My opinion is Maine, of course. To make my version of the confection, I am a true believer in using off-the-shelf Marshmallow Fluff for the filling, which gets sandwiched in between cocoa-flavored soft cookies.

MAKES 18 WHOOPIE PIES

FOR THE BATTER

8 tablespoons (115 g/1 stick) unsalted butter, at room temperature

1 cup (200 g) granulated sugar

1 large egg

1 teaspoon vanilla extract

1⅔ cups (205 g) all-purpose flour

⅔ cup (65 g) unsweetened cocoa powder

1 teaspoon baking soda

½ teaspoon kosher salt

1 cup (240 ml) milk

¾ cup (180 ml) buttermilk

FOR THE FILLING

8 tablespoons (115 g/1 stick) unsalted butter, at room temperature

2 cups (180 g) Marshmallow Fluff

1¼ cups (155 g) powdered sugar

1 teaspoon vanilla extract

1. Preheat the oven to 375°F (190°C). Line three 18-by-13-inch (46 by 33 cm) baking sheets with parchment paper.

2. Make the batter: In a stand mixer fitted with the paddle (or in a large bowl with a hand mixer), beat the butter and granulated sugar at medium speed until fluffy, about 3 minutes. Add the egg and vanilla and continue to mix, scraping down the sides of the bowl as necessary.

3. In a medium bowl, combine the flour, cocoa powder, baking soda, and salt. In a separate bowl, combine the milk and buttermilk. With the mixer running on low, add half of the flour mixture and half of the milk mixture to the bowl and mix until the dough comes together, about 2 minutes. Add the remaining flour and milk mixtures and mix until combined, about 2 minutes.

4. For each cookie, scoop 2 tablespoons of batter onto a parchment-lined baking sheet, spacing the scoops 2 inches (5 cm) apart so they'll have room to expand. You'll have about 12 scoops on each baking sheet.

5. Bake one sheet at a time for 10 minutes. Let the cookies cool on the pan for 5 minutes, then transfer to a wire rack to cool completely before finishing the recipe.

6. Make the filling: In a stand mixer fitted with the paddle (or in a large bowl with a hand mixer), whip the butter on medium speed until light and airy, about 1 minute. Add the Fluff, powdered sugar, and vanilla and continue beating until the mixture is thoroughly combined, about 3 minutes.

7. Return the cooled cookies to the parchment-lined baking sheets, at room temperature. Flip half of the cookies over so that the flat side is facing up and scoop 2 tablespoons of filling on top of each. Gently place the remaining cookie halves on top, flat side down, and give them a little squeeze so that they hold together.

8. Serve the whoopie pies on a platter. Store in an airtight container at room temperature for up to 2 days or in the refrigerator for up to 5 days.

BUCKWHEAT BROWN BUTTER CHOCOLATE CHIP COOKIES

If you asked one hundred Americans to name their favorite sweet, I'm pretty sure ninety-nine of them would vote for chocolate chip cookies. I make mine with buckwheat, an old-time favorite in Maine pantries. It's a crop that grows well in our short growing season and adds a toasty, nutty flavor to baked goods. The thought of these hearty cookies calls up a memory—or maybe it's just a daydream—of a small-town country store with well-worn wooden floorboards and an oak-and-glass display case full of cookies, cupcakes, and pies.

MAKES ABOUT 24 COOKIES

12 ounces (340 g/3 sticks) unsalted butter

3 cups (360 g) all-purpose flour

1½ cups (180 g) buckwheat flour

1½ teaspoons baking powder

1½ teaspoons baking soda

1 tablespoon kosher salt

2 cups (400 g) firmly packed light brown sugar

1½ cups (300 g) granulated sugar

2 large eggs

1 tablespoon vanilla extract

2¼ cups (340 g) semisweet chocolate chips

Flaky salt, for finishing

1. Preheat the oven to 325°F (160°C). Line two baking sheets with parchment paper.

2. Melt the butter in a small saucepan over medium heat, gently swirling it. The butter will turn light brown and have a nutty aroma after 2 to 3 minutes. Remove the saucepan from the heat and set aside to cool.

3. In a medium bowl, whisk together the all-purpose flour, buckwheat flour, baking powder, baking soda, and kosher salt. Set aside.

4. In a stand mixer fitted with the paddle, cream the cooled brown butter, brown sugar, and granulated sugar on medium speed until light and fluffy, 5 to 7 minutes.

5. Add the eggs and mix until just combined, about 1 minute. Add the vanilla and mix for 30 seconds. On low speed, gradually add the flour mixture and mix until combined, 1 to 2 minutes. Stir in the chocolate chips.

6. Using a ¼-cup (60 ml) measure or #16 ice cream scoop, portion scoops of dough 2 inches (5 cm) apart on the lined baking sheets. Lightly press the cookie balls to flatten them.

7. Bake for 12 minutes, or until the cookies look puffy and lightly golden.

8. Remove the baking sheets from the oven and sprinkle the cookies with flaky salt. Let them cool on the baking sheets for 10 minutes before transferring to a wire rack or serving plate. Store in an airtight container at room temperature for 5 to 7 days.

PEANUT BUTTER MISO COOKIES

Adding white miso to the batter of a peanut butter cookie produces a light touch of fermented tanginess and whole lot of umami. If you are a peanut butter cookie fan, this recipe will be a keeper.

MAKES ABOUT 24 COOKIES

- 10 ounces (285 g/2½ sticks) unsalted butter, at room temperature
- 2½ cups loosely packed (330 g) light brown sugar
- 1¼ cups (250 g) granulated sugar
- ¾ cup (200 g) white miso paste
- ⅔ cup (170 g) creamy peanut butter
- 2 large eggs
- 1 tablespoon vanilla extract
- 4¼ cups (530 g) all-purpose flour
- 1¾ teaspoons baking soda
- 1¼ teaspoons baking powder
- Flaky salt, for finishing

1. Preheat the oven to 325°F (160°C). Line two baking sheets with parchment paper.

2. In a stand mixer fitted with the paddle, cream the butter, brown sugar, and granulated sugar on medium speed until light and fluffy, 5 to 7 minutes. Add the miso and peanut butter and mix on low speed until just combined, scraping down the sides of the bowl as necessary, 1 to 2 minutes. Add the eggs, one at a time, beating well after each addition. Add the vanilla, mixing briefly to combine.

3. In a separate bowl, whisk together the flour, baking soda, and baking powder. On low speed, gradually add the flour mixture to the peanut butter mixture and mix until combined, about 2 minutes, scraping down the sides as necessary.

4. Using a ¼-cup (60 ml) measure or #16 ice cream scoop, portion scoops of dough 2 inches (5 cm) apart on the lined baking sheets. Lightly press the cookie balls to flatten them.

5. Bake for about 12 minutes, or until the cookies look puffy and lightly golden.

6. Remove the baking sheets from the oven and sprinkle the cookies with flaky salt. Let them cool on the baking sheets for 10 minutes before transferring to a wire rack or serving plate. The cookies will be soft when they are fresh out of the oven, but they will finish to a snappy consistency as they come to room temperature. Store in an airtight container at room temperature for up to 5 days.

BLACKBERRY CRUMBLE BARS

Crumble bars are a satisfying snack when you need a little something to keep you going on a summer hike or a long paddle in a canoe. These homemade bars are way less expensive than the ones you buy at the market. And no supermarket bar is going to deliver the flavor combination of blackberries and freshly picked mint. I particularly like using licorice mint (also known to home gardeners as anise hyssop), but the leaves of regular mint will also work. Mint brings out the wild freshness of ripe, plump, juicy blackberries. If you are taking the bars along for a car trip or summer adventure, wrap the individual bars in parchment or waxed paper.

MAKES 16 BARS

Softened unsalted butter or cooking spray, for the pan

1 quart (560 g) blackberries

¼ cup (50 g) granulated sugar

3 tablespoons roughly chopped licorice mint (aka anise hyssop) or regular mint

2 tablespoons cornstarch

Juice of 1 lemon

Kosher salt

1 cup (125 g) all-purpose flour

1 cup (85 g) quick-cooking oats

½ cup loosely packed (120 g) light brown sugar

Grated zest of 1 lemon

½ teaspoon baking soda

8 tablespoons (115 g/1 stick) unsalted butter, at room temperature, cubed

1. Preheat the oven to 350°F (180°C). Grease an 8-inch (20 cm) square or round baking pan with about 1 tablespoon softened butter or cooking spray.

2. Set aside a small handful of the blackberries for garnish. Then, in a deep saucepan, combine the blackberries, granulated sugar, mint, cornstarch, lemon juice, and a pinch of salt. Stir over medium heat until the mixture comes to a boil. Reduce the heat to low and stir as needed so the mixture doesn't stick to the bottom of the pan. Cook until the mixture thickens to coat the back of a spoon, 8 to 10 minutes. Set aside to cool.

3. In a medium bowl, combine the flour, oats, brown sugar, lemon zest, baking soda, and ¼ teaspoon salt. Mix well using your hands, then add the butter and mix until the bits of butter are the size of peas.

4. Spread about three-quarters of the crumble mixture into the prepared baking pan and press down using your fingertips to flatten the mixture and create the crust.

5. Bake for 10 minutes. Remove from the oven and set aside to cool for 5 minutes. Leave the oven on.

6. Pour the blackberry mixture over the crust and spread it around evenly with a rubber spatula (see photos, page 282). Sprinkle the top with the remaining crumble and the reserved fresh blackberries. Return the pan to the oven and bake for 30 minutes, until bubbling and lightly browned.

7. Set the pan on a wire rack to cool completely. Cut the blackberry crumble into 16 squares. Store in the refrigerator for 5 to 7 days or individually wrapped in the freezer for up to 3 months.

RHUBARB GALETTE

Every year as the weather starts to turn mild, the first fresh-from-the-garden ingredient suitable for pie making is rhubarb. I wonder who first had the inspired idea that rhubarb—which is so tart it can seriously pucker you—would be a good main ingredient in a dessert. The tartness of the rhubarb contrasted with the sweetness of the sugar works beautifully. This rustic-looking galette is a good way to slide into pie-making season. A scoop of ice cream on top is always a good idea.

SERVES 8

FOR THE CRUST

2 cups (250 g) all-purpose flour, plus more for dusting

½ teaspoon kosher salt

8 ounces (225 g/2 sticks) cold unsalted butter

8 to 10 tablespoons (120 to 150 ml) cold water, as needed

FOR THE FILLING

1 pound (455 g) rhubarb, cut into ½-inch (13 mm) slices

⅔ cup (135 g) sugar

2 tablespoons cornstarch

1 tablespoon fresh lemon juice

2 teaspoons grated peeled fresh ginger

Grated zest of 1 orange

Egg wash: 1 egg beaten with 1 tablespoon milk

1. Make the crust: In a large bowl, combine the flour and salt. Using a box grater, grate in the cold butter and mix by hand to incorporate it. Take care not to overwork the dough because you want the butter to remain in pea-size pieces. Add the cold water slowly and mix by hand until the dough barely comes together. It will be shaggy; no kneading needed. Cover the dough and let rest in the refrigerator for 30 minutes.

2. On a floured work surface, roll out the dough into a rectangle, roughly 12 inches by 8 inches (30 by 20 cm). With a long side facing you, fold the right third over the center and then fold the left third over that, just as if you were folding a business letter. Rotate the dough 90 degrees, then roll it out and fold it again in the same manner. Cover the dough with a kitchen towel and refrigerate for 15 minutes. Repeat this process of rolling, folding, and chilling twice more.

3. Meanwhile, make the filling: In a large bowl, toss the rhubarb with ⅓ cup (65 g) of the sugar and set aside for 10 minutes. Drain the rhubarb and discard the liquid. Stir in the remaining ⅓ cup (65 g) sugar, the cornstarch, lemon juice, ginger, and orange zest.

4. Preheat the oven to 375°F (190°C). Line a baking sheet with parchment paper.

5. On a floured work surface, roll out the dough into a rough round ⅛ inch (3 mm) thick. Place a 12-inch (30 cm) dinner plate upside down on the dough, lightly pressing down so that the dinner plate leaves its outline in the dough when you remove the plate. Set the plate aside and make six 1-inch (2.5 cm) slits around the edge of the rough round. Transfer the dough to the lined baking sheet.

6. Place the rhubarb mixture in the center of the rolled-out dough and, using a spatula, spread the mixture evenly, leaving about 1 inch (2.5 cm) of the circular pattern you traced with the dinner plate as a border (which will allow for neatly folding the dough where you've created the slits). Fold the fringed edges of the dough over to enclose the galette. Brush the crust of the galette with the egg wash.

7. Bake for 30 minutes. The crust will be nicely golden (it may need another minute or two in the oven to achieve this color).

8. Let the galette cool for at least 20 minutes on a wire rack, then lift the galette by the parchment and transfer it to a flat surface. Insert a large spatula between the parchment and the galette. Lift slightly to tilt the galette in order to remove the parchment. Let cool for 30 minutes more before cutting and serving. Store, covered, at room temperature for up to 1 day or in the refrigerator for up to 5 days.

BLUEBERRY FOOL PAVLOVA

If you say the word *dessert* and ask me what I imagine, I always picture this pavlova as if shimmering into life by the wave of a wizard's wand. It checks all the boxes that I want in a dessert: crispness, from the light-as-air meringue; creaminess, from the whipped cream; and sweetness, from the blueberry puree. Lightly mixing whipped cream and puree, so that veins of blue run through the white cream, makes it what the British call a fool. You'll top it with the sweet pop and light tang of fresh blueberries, ideally just picked from a Maine blueberry barren.

SERVES 6

FOR THE INFUSED CREAM

2 cups (480 ml) heavy cream

2 tablespoons chopped licorice mint (aka anise hyssop) or regular mint

FOR THE MERINGUES

4 egg whites, at room temperature

½ cup (100 g) granulated sugar

½ cup (60 g) powdered sugar

½ teaspoon cream of tartar

FOR THE BLUEBERRY PUREE

2 cups (290 g) blueberries, fresh or thawed frozen

¼ cup (50 g) granulated sugar

2 tablespoons fresh lemon juice

1 teaspoon grated lemon zest

Pinch of kosher salt

ingredients continue

1. Make the infused cream: In a deep saucepan, warm the heavy cream for a few minutes over medium-low heat. Remove from the heat, add the mint, and steep for 2 hours. Strain, discarding the mint, and refrigerate for 30 minutes.

2. Meanwhile, make the meringues: Preheat the oven to 200°F (90°C). Line a baking sheet with parchment paper.

3. In a stand mixer fitted with the whisk, beat the egg whites on medium speed until they are quite frothy, about 2 minutes. Add the granulated sugar and continue whisking until soft peaks start to form, then increase the mixer speed to high and beat until stiff peaks form, about 5 minutes. Add the powdered sugar and cream of tartar and briefly mix to incorporate. The mixture should be glossy and smooth; you should not be able to feel any grittiness if you rub a little between your thumb and finger.

4. Dollop the meringue in 6 equal portions onto the lined baking sheet. Using the back of a tablespoon, make a depression in each meringue (see photo, page 289). Transfer the baking sheet to the oven.

5. Bake for 1½ hours, or until the meringues are firm and dry. They should be light and airy and release easily from the baking sheet. Set aside to cool for 30 minutes.

6. While the meringues are baking, make the blueberry puree: In a deep saucepan, combine the blueberries, sugar, lemon juice,

FOR ASSEMBLY

3 tablespoons powdered sugar

2 tablespoons fresh blueberries, for topping

lemon zest, and salt. Stir with a wooden spoon and bring the mixture to a boil over medium-high heat. Immediately reduce the heat to medium and simmer until the berries are quite soft, about 6 minutes. You may need to adjust the heat so that the blueberries don't sputter outside the pan.

7. Transfer the blueberry mixture to a blender. Starting on low speed so as not to spatter and then increasing to medium speed, puree the mixture until smooth, 1 to 2 minutes. Using a fine-mesh sieve, strain the mixture into a small bowl and set aside.

8. To assemble: In a bowl, using an electric mixer or a whisk, whip the chilled infused cream and powdered sugar until medium stiff peaks form, 3 to 5 minutes. Gently fold half of the blueberry puree into the whipped cream. You want to see veins of blueberries running through the white cream. Reserve the rest of the puree to spoon over the meringue.

9. To serve, place the meringues on separate plates, spoon the remaining blueberry puree into the middle of the meringues, and finish with the whipped cream mixture and whole berries. Best to serve immediately, but it will keep in the refrigerator for up to 3 days.

ROASTED WHITE CHOCOLATE MOUSSE

White chocolate is made from cacao, the same raw ingredient used in all chocolates. The difference is that white chocolate leaves out the dark solids that give chocolate its deep brown color. Because white chocolate includes only light-colored cocoa butter, oven-roasting the morsels allows them to develop a beautiful dark amber color, which looks like rich, creamy butterscotch when whipped into a mousse.

SERVES 6

- 12 ounces (340 g) white chocolate morsels or chips
- 2 cups (480 ml) heavy cream
- 2 tablespoons (30 g) unsalted butter
- 2 egg whites (see Note)
- ¼ cup (50 g) sugar
- Honeycomb Crumble (recipe follows)
- 1 cup (125 g) raspberries

1. Preheat the oven to 250°F (120°C). Line a baking sheet with parchment paper.

2. Spread the white chocolate morsels on the lined baking sheet and roast, lightly stirring every 5 minutes with a wooden spoon, until the chocolate takes on an amber color, about 30 minutes. The white chocolate won't be fully melted or runny but melted enough for what is needed.

3. Meanwhile, bring 2 cups (480 ml) water to a boil in the bottom of a double boiler over medium-high heat.

4. Remove the baking sheet from the oven and transfer the white chocolate to the top of the double boiler. Add ½ cup (120 ml) of the heavy cream and the butter. Stir from time to time until the mixture softens and partially melts, 8 to 10 minutes. Remove the top of the double boiler with the chocolate mixture and set it aside to cool.

5. In a stand mixer fitted with the whisk, whip the remaining 1½ cups (360 ml) heavy cream on medium speed until soft peaks form, about 3 minutes. Using a rubber spatula, transfer the whipped cream to a large bowl.

6. Clean and dry the bowl and whisk attachment of the stand mixer. Using the whisk attachment, beat the egg whites on medium speed and slowly add the sugar. The mixture will begin to froth. Continue mixing until soft peaks form, 5 to 7 minutes.

7. Remove the bowl from the stand mixer, gently fold the white chocolate into the beaten egg whites, and then fold in the whipped cream. Transfer the finished mousse to dessert bowls or glasses and refrigerate for at least 2 hours and preferably overnight.

8. To serve, sprinkle bits of crumbled honeycomb over the mousse and top with fresh raspberries. Store the mousse, covered, in the refrigerator for up to 4 days.

NOTE: This recipe incorporates raw egg whites, so use quality eggs, preferably from your local farmer.

Honeycomb Crumble

MAKES ABOUT
4 CUPS (100 G)

Softened butter or cooking spray, for the pan
1½ cups (300 g) sugar
¼ cup (60 ml) maple syrup
1 tablespoon baking soda

Add a bit of sweet crunch to your desserts by making a honeycomb—a baking term for a mix of sugars, water, and baking soda that hardens into a sugar cake with an airy structure. Use it crumbled on top of puddings, ice cream, and mousse.

1. Butter a baking sheet and line it with parchment paper. Butter the parchment as well. You could also use baking spray instead of butter.

2. In a deep saucepan, combine the sugar, maple syrup, and ¼ cup (60 ml) water. Warm the mixture over medium heat until a candy thermometer reads 300°F (149°C). Remove the pan from the heat and whisk in the baking soda; it will foam up. Immediately pour the mixture onto the prepared baking sheet and set aside to cool to room temperature. The mixture will harden.

3. Once cool, break the honeycomb into smaller pieces. Store the honeycomb in an airtight container at room temperature for up to 2 weeks.

APPLE AND WALNUT FRANGIPANE TART

One of the most fun-to-say food words is *frangipane*. It could be the name of a clown in the circus. Where did it come from? Like a lot of food origin stories, it's a toss-up. I'm going with the story that credits Marquis Muzio Frangipani, an Italian nobleman who invented a perfume that carried the scent of almonds. In his honor, the sweet almond paste used in pastry came to be known as frangipane. For my frangipane, I make a walnut paste that goes well with apples and pears.

SERVES 8

FOR THE CRUST

6 tablespoons (85 g/¾ stick) cold unsalted butter

¼ cup (50 g) sugar

1½ cups (190 g) all-purpose flour, plus more for dusting

¾ cup (75 g) rye flour

½ teaspoon kosher salt

2 large eggs

2 tablespoons ice water

FOR THE FILLING

Juice of 1 lemon

4 Granny Smith apples

1 cup (120 g) chopped walnuts

10½ tablespoons (150 g) unsalted butter, at room temperature

½ cup (100 g) sugar

3 large eggs

1 teaspoon vanilla extract

½ teaspoon ground cinnamon

1. Make the crust: In a stand mixer fitted with the paddle, cream the butter and sugar on medium-low speed until light and fluffy, about 2 minutes. With the motor still running, add the all-purpose flour, rye flour, and salt and mix until the mixture resembles coarse bread crumbs, scraping down the sides of the bowl from time to time.

2. In a separate bowl, beat the eggs and ice water together. With the mixer on medium-low speed, add the egg mixture to the bowl. Continue beating until the dough just comes together. Remove the dough to a floured work surface. Using your hands, flatten and shape the dough into a disk. Wrap the dough in plastic and refrigerate for 30 minutes.

3. Remove the dough from the refrigerator and transfer to a lightly floured work surface. Using a rolling pin, roll out the dough into a rough round about ⅛ inch (3 mm) thick and 12½ inches (32 cm) in diameter—a little larger than a 9½-inch (24 cm) tart pan with a removable bottom. Using the rolling pin, lift the dough from the work surface and gently lay it into the tart pan, pressing the edge of the dough into the sides of the pan. Pass a rolling pin over the top of the pan to cut off any excess dough (see photos, page 295). Press the dough around the edges of the pan again so the trimmed edge of the dough sits slightly above the edge of the pan. Refrigerate for at least 20 minutes before assembling the tart.

¼ teaspoon ground nutmeg

⅔ cup (80 g) all-purpose flour, sifted

½ teaspoon baking powder

1 cup (240 ml) apple cider

Ice cream, for serving (optional)

4. Meanwhile, preheat the oven to 375°F (190°C).

5. Prepare the filling: In a bowl, combine 1 quart (960 ml) water and the lemon juice. Using a sharp vegetable peeler, peel the apples top to bottom. Core and halve the apples and slice them into half-moons about ¼ inch (6 mm) thick. Place the apple slices in the bowl (the acid in the lemon juice will keep them from turning brown). Set aside.

6. Toast the walnuts on a small baking sheet or in a cast-iron skillet in the oven for about 8 minutes. When you smell a nutty aroma—it could be sooner than 8 minutes—remove the nuts from the oven. Transfer the toasted walnuts to a food processor and grind to coarse bits.

7. In a stand mixer fitted with the paddle, beat the butter and sugar on medium speed until light and fluffy, about 3 minutes. Add the eggs, one at a time, beating until they are well incorporated. Add the ground toasted walnuts, vanilla, cinnamon, and nutmeg and mix for 15 seconds. With the mixer still running, add the sifted flour and baking powder. Mix until combined, 1 to 2 minutes.

8. Remove the tart shell from the refrigerator and, using a spatula, spread the walnut filling evenly over the bottom of the tart. Drain the apple slices and arrange them on top of the filling, lightly pressing them into the frangipane as you lay them out.

9. Place the tart pan on a baking sheet and bake until the frangipane is puffed up and the apples are lightly brown, about 45 minutes. Let the tart cool in the pan on a wire rack for 30 minutes, then unmold.

10. Meanwhile, in a small saucepan, cook the apple cider over medium heat until reduced to a syrupy consistency, about 15 minutes.

11. Brush the warm tart with the cider glaze and let cool for 1 hour before serving. A scoop of vanilla ice cream would be a welcome addition. Store any leftovers in an airtight container in the refrigerator for up to 4 days.

SPRUCE TIP GRANITA WITH FRESH BERRIES

Every year, the spruce trees in our ancient evergreen forest sprout new tips for their boughs. The tiny tips have a sunny light-green color that contrasts beautifully with the deep green of the old year's needles. When the needles are young and tender, we forage them for this refreshing dessert. The tender tips have a citrusy taste and the clean aroma of the forest on a fresh April day. I freeze the tips until berry season to make a refreshing granita. The granita is scraped and shaved and piled with some fresh berries and mint leaves in a parfait glass.

SERVES 4

1 cup (200 g) sugar
1 cup (60 g) frozen spruce tips
Grated zest and juice of ½ lemon
1 cup (about 150 g) fresh berries

1. In a deep medium saucepan, combine 3 cups (720 ml) water and the sugar and set over medium-high heat, stirring to dissolve. Remove the saucepan from the heat. Add the spruce tips, lemon zest, and lemon juice and steep for 30 minutes.

2. Strain the liquid into a shallow container and place it in the freezer. After 30 minutes, check on the mixture. As the liquid starts to crystallize, scrape it with a fork to begin to break up the ice crystals. Repeat this process of scraping the ice with a fork three or four times, breaking up the ice crystals but not turning them into slush.

3. To serve, add some granita to a parfait glass or dessert cup. Top with some berries, then another layer of granita and berries.

SAKE-POACHED PEARS

When I first bought my place on Goose Cove, I planted an orchard: apple, plum, cherry, and pear trees. Every year at summer's end, I look forward to poaching my own Goose Cove pears in red wine and mulling spices—a classic of French country cuisine. This variation is a Japanese twist on the French original. You'll poach the pears in sake, pear juice, and yuzu juice, the latter made from an Asian fruit that tastes like a combination of lemon and grapefruit. The sweet flavor of the poaching liquid is pulled together by the aromatic notes of crystallized ginger, vanilla bean, and honey. The flesh of the poached pear takes on an almost alabaster glow.

SERVES 4

FOR THE POACHED PEARS

3 tablespoons fresh lemon juice

4 Bosc or Bartlett pears, or 8 Seckel (sugar) pears

3 cups (720 ml) filtered sake (1 standard bottle)

1 cup (240 ml) pear juice or apple juice

6 tablespoons (90 ml) yuzu juice

2 tablespoons honey

1 teaspoon roughly chopped crystallized ginger

Pinch of kosher salt

1 vanilla bean, split lengthwise and seeds scraped out

FOR THE CRÈME FRAÎCHE TOPPING

1 cup (240 ml) crème fraîche or sour cream

2 tablespoons sugar

1. Poach the pears: In a bowl, combine 1 quart (960 ml) water and the lemon juice. Using a sharp vegetable peeler, peel the pears top to bottom, leaving them whole, with stems attached and the core intact. As you peel them, place the pears in the bowl (the acid in the lemon juice will keep them from turning brown).

2. Remove the pears from the bowl and transfer them to a nonreactive pot. Add the sake, pear juice, yuzu juice, honey, ginger, salt, and vanilla seeds (add the scraped pod as well). Bring to a boil over high heat, then reduce the heat to maintain a gentle simmer, cover with the lid slightly ajar, and cook until the pears are tender, 20 to 30 minutes. Test for doneness by inserting a thin skewer or cake tester into a pear; if you can penetrate it easily, they are done.

3. Remove the pears to a bowl and set them aside. Heat the poaching liquid over medium-high heat and reduce until it has a syrupy consistency. Measure out 2 tablespoons of the syrup and set aside for the topping. Pour the remaining syrup over the pears and refrigerate for at least 2 hours or overnight. (Store the poached pears in their syrup for up to 5 days in the refrigerator.)

4. Make the crème fraîche topping: In a small bowl, whisk together the crème fraîche, sugar, and reserved poaching syrup.

5. To serve, put a dollop of the sweetened crème fraîche in a shallow soup bowl and set a chilled pear on top.

BASICS

Stocks and Broths
302

Aiolis
307

Refrigerator Pickles
311

STOCKS AND BROTHS

Whenever I have leftovers or scraps that don't make it into a savory recipe, my goal is to rescue the flavor that's locked into them before they go into the compost bin. Pan-roasting, long simmering, straining, and finally reducing the liquid for more convenient storage creates stocks and broths that are powerful first steps for making soups, stews, braises, sauces, and gravies. They add a depth of flavor that elevates pasta, risotto, and all kinds of beans, or just about anything.

ROASTED VEGETABLE STOCK

In most stocks, the vegetables are merely supporting members, but here, by caramelizing a stock of just vegetables, they become the main players. The result is a broth with a nutty, sweet quality—plus, it's 100% vegan!

MAKES ABOUT 4 QUARTS (3.84 L)

1 pound (455 g) celery, roughly chopped (including the leaves)

1 pound (455 g) carrots, scrubbed and roughly chopped

1 pound (455 g) onions, peeled and quartered

3 large leeks, white parts only, well rinsed and roughly chopped

2 heads garlic, unpeeled, halved horizontally

8 thyme sprigs

4 bay leaves

1 cup (50 g) chopped fresh flat-leaf parsley

2 tablespoons whole black peppercorns

2 tablespoons grapeseed or canola oil

1. Preheat the oven to 400°F (200°C).

2. In a large bowl, toss together the vegetables, garlic, herbs, peppercorns, and oil. Transfer the mixture to a roasting pan and roast until the vegetables start to caramelize or turn golden brown, about 20 minutes. Stir from time to time for even browning.

3. Transfer the contents of the roasting pan to a stockpot. Place the roasting pan over high heat, pour in ½ cup (120 ml) water, and deglaze the pan, scraping up the caramelized bits on the bottom. Add this to the stockpot, along with 4 quarts (3.84 L) water. Bring to a boil over high heat, then reduce the heat to low and simmer for 1 hour.

4. Line a fine-mesh sieve with cheesecloth. Strain the stock into a large bowl, pressing gently on the solids to get every last bit of flavor (discard the solids). When the stock has cooled, store it in 1-quart (960 ml) containers in the refrigerator for up to 4 days or in the freezer for up to 6 months.

FISH BROTH

Fumet, the fish stock of classic French cuisine, is paired here with dashi for a powerful, elegant broth with great depth of flavor. Caramelizing the vegetables adds another layer of flavor. The fish, however, doesn't want to be roasted or browned (the broth would get cloudy if you roasted the fish and bones). Instead, it is simmered with the caramelized vegetables. This broth is spectacular with dumplings or swimming in a wide soup plate with clams, mussels, shrimp, or any white-fleshed fish fillet.

MAKES ABOUT 4 QUARTS (3.84 L)

3 pounds (1.4 kg) halibut bones or bones of other white-fleshed fish
8 tablespoons (115 g/1 stick) unsalted butter
1 large onion, roughly chopped
2 large leeks, well rinsed and roughly chopped
3 celery ribs, roughly chopped (including the leaves)
1 fennel bulb, roughly chopped
1 (2-inch/5 cm) piece fresh ginger, peeled and sliced
4 garlic cloves, roughly chopped
2 tablespoons white miso paste
1 cup (240 ml) sake
1 teaspoon whole black peppercorns
1 cup (35 g) dried mushrooms, thoroughly brushed and rinsed to remove grit
¼ cup (3 g) bonito flakes
3 (6-inch/15 cm) pieces kombu
¾ cup (180 ml) mirin
½ cup (120 ml) tamari
2 tablespoons fresh lime juice
Kosher salt

1. Soak the fish bones in cold water for 30 minutes.

2. Melt the butter in a nonreactive Dutch oven or a stockpot over medium heat until it foams. Add the onion, leeks, celery, fennel, ginger, and garlic. Cook until the onions are translucent, about 8 minutes.

3. Add the miso and stir to coat the vegetables. Cook until the vegetables get sticky on the bottom of the pot, 2 to 3 minutes. Drain the fish bones, add them to the pot, and cook for 10 minutes.

4. Pour in the sake and deglaze the pot, scraping up any browned bits on the bottom. Add 4 quarts (3.84 L) water and the peppercorns, mushrooms, and bonito flakes. Simmer gently for 1 hour.

5. Add the kombu and simmer gently for another 30 minutes to extract all the flavor. Don't let the liquid boil or the broth will turn cloudy.

6. Line a fine-mesh sieve with cheesecloth and strain the liquid into a large bowl, pressing gently on the solids to get every last bit of flavor (discard the solids). Return the liquid to the pot. Add the mirin, tamari, and lime juice. Season to taste with salt. When the broth has cooled, store it in 1-quart (960 ml) containers in the refrigerator for up to 4 days or in the freezer for up to 6 months.

TIDAL BROTH

I think of this recipe as the heavy artillery of umami-fueled flavor building, so whenever you cook lobsters, don't ever throw away the shells. Make this stock right away or freeze the heads and shells until you're ready. This broth, a combination of classic Italian lobster brodo and the prime ingredients of dashi, is foundational for building flavor in your recipes. Use it for poaching fish, for steaming clams or mussels, for making risotto, paella, and bouillabaisse, and to fortify sauces.

MAKES ABOUT 4 QUARTS (3.84 L)

Heads and shells of 3 or 4 cooked lobsters (see Note)

2 tablespoons grapeseed or canola oil

8 tablespoons (115 g/1 stick) unsalted butter

2 leeks, halved lengthwise, well rinsed, and thinly sliced

1 large onion, roughly chopped

3 celery ribs, roughly chopped (including the leaves)

1 medium fennel bulb, roughly chopped

1 (2-inch/5 cm) piece fresh ginger, peeled and roughly chopped

4 garlic cloves, roughly chopped

¼ cup (60 g) tomato paste

2 tablespoons white miso paste

1 cup (240 ml) sake

1 cup (35 g) dried mushrooms, thoroughly brushed and rinsed to remove grit

3 (6-inch/15 cm) pieces kombu

¾ cup (180 ml) mirin

½ cup (120 ml) tamari

2 tablespoons fresh lime juice

Kosher salt

1. Break off the heads of the cooked lobsters and split them in half with a large chef's knife. Discard the green stuff in the head and body cavity (tomalley). Break up the rest of the shells with a chef's knife or briefly pulse the shells in a food processor. You aren't chopping the shells into tiny pieces, but you want to break them up just enough that you can more easily roast off and lightly caramelize all the surface areas of the lobster shells and heads.

2. Warm the oil in a large skillet over medium-high heat until it starts to shimmer. Add the split and cleaned heads and lobster shells. Using tongs or a large wooden spoon, turn the shells as they lightly brown. Don't crowd the pan. You want as much shell as possible to be exposed to the heated pan, so you may need to work in batches. Cook until browned, about 3 minutes. Remove the lobster shells to a stockpot or a nonreactive Dutch oven.

3. Melt the butter in the same large skillet over medium-high heat until it starts to foam. Add the leeks, onion, celery, fennel, ginger, and garlic. Cook until the vegetables soften, 5 to 7 minutes.

4. Add the tomato paste and miso, stirring to coat the vegetables. Cook until the mixture gets sticky on the bottom of the pan, 2 to 3 minutes. Add the sake and deglaze the pan, scraping up the browned bits. Continue cooking until the sake is reduced by half. Transfer the contents of the skillet to the stockpot or Dutch oven. Add 4 quarts (3.84 L) water, the mushrooms, and kombu and turn the heat to low. Simmer for 30 minutes.

5. Line a fine-mesh sieve with cheesecloth and strain the liquid into a large bowl, pressing gently on the solids to get every last bit of flavor (discard the solids). Return the liquid to the stockpot or Dutch oven. Add the mirin, tamari, and lime juice. Season to taste with salt. When the broth has cooled, store it in 1-quart (960 ml) containers in the refrigerator for up to 4 days or in the freezer for up to 6 months.

NOTE: If shrimp shells are all you have, they will work for this recipe; use the shells from 2 to 3 pounds (roughly 1 to 1.5 kg) shrimp.

ROASTED CHICKEN STOCK

If there is one universal stock that works for nearly everything (except for vegetarian meals, of course), it is chicken stock. It is deeply savory yet not overpowering and is economical to make. Uncooked chicken wings, leftover chicken bones, and odd bits like necks and backs are relatively inexpensive and full of flavor. Roasting these chicken parts creates the irresistible flavor that high heat develops on any meat product (food scientists call this the Maillard reaction and it is the secret to so much of what we love about grilled meats). Risotto, paella, bouillabaisse, dumplings, soups, and all kinds of dried beans take nicely to chicken stock.

MAKES ABOUT 4 QUARTS (3.84 L)

2 pounds (900 g) chicken wings, plus any unused or leftover chicken parts and bones
4 celery ribs, roughly chopped (including the leaves)
3 carrots, roughly chopped
2 onions, roughly chopped
2 leeks, white parts only, well rinsed and roughly diced
1 head garlic, unpeeled, halved horizontally
4 thyme sprigs
4 bay leaves
Handful of parsley stems
1 tablespoon whole black peppercorns
2 tablespoons grapeseed or canola oil
½ cup (120 ml) dry white wine

1. Preheat the oven to 400°F (200°C).

2. Place the chicken wings and any leftover chicken parts and bones in a roasting pan and roast for 20 minutes, stirring after 10 minutes.

3. Meanwhile, in a large bowl, toss the vegetables, garlic, herbs, and peppercorns with the oil to coat.

4. Add the vegetable-herb mixture to the roasting pan and roast until the vegetables start to caramelize or turn golden brown, about 20 minutes. Scrape and stir the vegetables from time to time for even browning.

5. Transfer the contents of the roasting pan to a stockpot. Set the roasting pan over high heat, pour in the white wine, and deglaze the pan, scraping up the caramelized bits on the bottom. Add this to the stockpot, along with 4 quarts (3.84 L) water. Bring to a boil over high heat, then reduce the heat to low and simmer for 3 hours.

6. Line a fine-mesh sieve with cheesecloth and strain the stock into a large bowl, pressing gently on the solids to get every last bit of chicken flavor (discard the solids). When the stock has cooled, store it in 1-quart (960 ml) containers in the refrigerator for up to 4 days or in the freezer for up to 6 months.

PARMESAN BROTH

Western cooking has utilized umami flavors for ages. Among the ingredients that are high in umami are anchovies, seaweed, tomatoes, and all kinds of hard cheeses—especially Parmesan. "What does it do?" you might ask. Long story short, umami makes good-tasting things more delicious. Keep your hard Parmesan rinds in the freezer until you have enough to make this broth. You can also toss a rind into soups, braises, gravies, or sauces and it will bring out savory flavor and add body.

MAKES ABOUT 4 QUARTS (3.84 L)

2 tablespoons (30 g) unsalted butter
2 tablespoons olive oil
1 medium onion, roughly chopped
1 head garlic, unpeeled, halved horizontally
1 pound (455 g) Parmesan rinds
Handful of parsley sprigs
3 thyme sprigs
2 bay leaves
1 teaspoon whole black peppercorns

1. Melt the butter in the oil in a Dutch oven or stockpot over medium heat until it foams. Add the onion and garlic and cook until the onion softens, 6 to 8 minutes.

2. Add the Parmesan rinds, parsley, thyme, bay leaves, and peppercorns and stir to coat. Pour in 4 quarts (3.84 L) water and bring to a boil. Reduce the heat and allow the broth to bubble at a low simmer for 2 hours, stirring occasionally to prevent the cheese rinds from sticking to the bottom of the pot.

3. Line a fine-mesh sieve with cheesecloth. Strain the broth into a large bowl, pressing gently on the solids to get every last bit of flavor (discard the solids). When the broth has cooled, store it in 1-quart (960 ml) containers in the refrigerator for up to 4 days or in the freezer for up to 6 months.

AIOLIS

My go-to flavor and texture booster is aioli. Like mayonnaise, it is an emulsion (a mixture of two liquids that don't normally mix), and the way an aioli comes together is a bit magical. The eggs should always be at room temperature and the oil should be added slowly at first. You can make an aioli by hand with a whisk, but it comes together much more quickly in a food processor or blender. The result is pleasantly creamy in texture and tangy in taste.

Aioli makes each mouthful of whatever you put it on more flavorful. You like a squeeze of lemon on fried fish? Try Grilled Lemon Aioli (below). Or maybe you like tartar sauce? Then try the Dill Cornichon Aioli (page 308). And once you've got the hang of it, by all means go with your own variations.

NOTE: If not using it immediately, you can store aioli in an airtight container in the refrigerator for up to 4 days.

GRILLED LEMON AIOLI

This aioli is delicious with fish, asparagus, artichokes, and just about any sandwich where you would use mayonnaise.

MAKES ABOUT 1¼ CUPS (300 G)

2 lemons
1 large egg, at room temperature
1 egg yolk, at room temperature
½ teaspoon kosher salt, or to taste
1 cup (240 ml) grapeseed or canola oil

1. Prepare an outdoor grill to high heat or, if cooking inside, preheat a ridged grill pan or skillet over high heat for a few minutes.

2. Grate the zest from the lemons and set the zest aside. Halve the lemons horizontally and place the halves face down on the hot grill or grill pan and char until the cut side begins to blacken, about 5 minutes. Remove from the grill or grill pan. When the lemons have cooled enough to handle, juice them and strain out the seeds and bits.

3. In a food processor or blender, combine the whole egg and egg yolk and blend for 30 seconds. Add the lemon zest, lemon juice, and salt. Blend for another 30 seconds. With the machine running, slowly drizzle in the oil until the mixture starts to thicken, at which point you can pour in the rest of the oil in a slightly steadier stream. If the aioli is a little too thick after the oil is incorporated, drizzle in about 1 tablespoon of water to loosen it a bit.

MISO BROWN BUTTER AIOLI

Use with seared scallops, crab salad, hash brown potatoes, eggs, grilled breads, and vegetables.

MAKES ABOUT 1¼ CUPS (300 G)

8 tablespoons (115 g/1 stick) unsalted butter
1 large egg, at room temperature
1 egg yolk, at room temperature
Grated zest and juice of 1 lemon
1 tablespoon white miso paste
½ teaspoon kosher salt, or to taste
1 cup (240 ml) grapeseed or canola oil

1. Melt the butter in a small saucepan over medium heat, swirling or whisking so that the butter solids don't burn. The butter will start to foam and then turn golden brown. Remove the butter from the heat and pour it into a medium bowl. Set it aside briefly to cool to room temperature before proceeding.

2. In a food processor or blender, combine the whole egg and egg yolk and blend for 30 seconds. Add the lemon zest, lemon juice, miso, and salt and blend for another 30 seconds. With the machine running, slowly drizzle in the oil until the mixture starts to thicken, at which point you can pour in the rest of the oil in a slightly steadier stream. Finally, pour in the brown butter and blend. If the aioli is a little too thick after the oil and butter are incorporated, drizzle in about 1 tablespoon water to loosen it a bit.

DILL CORNICHON AIOLI

Great with fried chicken, sandwiches, egg salad, dips, crab cakes, and salmon.

MAKES ABOUT 2 CUPS (480 G)

1 large egg, at room temperature
1 egg yolk, at room temperature
Grated zest and juice of 1 lemon
1 tablespoon cornichon pickle brine
½ teaspoon kosher salt, or to taste
1 cup (240 ml) grapeseed or canola oil
¼ cup (13 g) fresh dill
¼ cup (40 g) roughly chopped cornichons

In a food processor or blender, combine the whole egg and egg yolk and blend for 30 seconds. Add the lemon zest, lemon juice, cornichon brine, and salt and blend for another 30 seconds. With the machine running, slowly drizzle in the oil until the mixture starts to thicken, at which point you can pour in the rest of the oil in a slightly steadier stream. If the aioli is a little too thick after the oil is incorporated, drizzle in about 1 tablespoon water to loosen it a bit. Add the dill and cornichons and pulse just a few times; you want to incorporate the dill and cornichons but still have little chunks in the aioli.

SAFFRON AIOLI

People often shy away from using saffron because it is expensive, but the amount used in this recipe is scant. Saffron aioli pumps up the flavor of what you're serving but won't break your credit score. Try it with seafood, roasted potatoes or meats, hard-boiled eggs, crudités, and bouillabaisse.

MAKES ABOUT 1¼ CUPS (300 G)

1 large egg, at room temperature
1 egg yolk, at room temperature
Grated zest and juice of 1 lemon
2 garlic cloves, minced or grated
1½ teaspoons loosely packed saffron threads
½ teaspoon kosher salt, or to taste
1 cup (240 ml) grapeseed or canola oil

In a food processor or blender, combine the whole egg and egg yolk and blend for 30 seconds. Add the lemon zest, lemon juice, garlic, saffron, and salt and blend for another 30 seconds. With the machine running, slowly drizzle in the oil until the mixture starts to thicken, at which point you can pour in the rest of the oil in a slightly steadier stream. If the aioli is a little too thick after the oil is incorporated, drizzle in about 1 tablespoon water to loosen it a bit.

REFRIGERATOR PICKLES

It's a long time between when the last apple is picked in October and the first asparagus shows up in April, but Mainers have a long tradition of preserving vegetables by making pickles. What I make are usually referred to as refrigerator pickles (or quick pickles), because instead of sealing them in sterilized jars, I store them in the fridge and they can be enjoyed as early as the next day and for up to 2 weeks.

BASIC PICKLE BRINE

MAKES 2 QUARTS (1.92 L)

2 cups (480 ml) rice vinegar
¾ cup (150 g) sugar
2 teaspoons kosher salt

1. In a nonreactive saucepan, combine 1½ cups (360 ml) water with the vinegar, the sugar, and salt. Bring to a low simmer over medium heat and cook, stirring a few times, until the sugar completely dissolves, about 5 minutes.

2. Remove the saucepan from the heat and use immediately to make pickles or allow it to cool and store in an airtight container in the refrigerator for up to 2 weeks. Unless otherwise directed, reheat the brine before using.

PICKLED BABY BEETS

MAKES 1 PINT (480 ML)

8 ounces (225 g) baby beets
½ teaspoon fennel seeds
1 bay leaf
Basic Pickle Brine (see above), hot

Scrub and trim the beets. Using a mandoline or a knife, cut the beets into slices ¼ inch (6 mm) thick. Transfer the slices to a 1-pint (480 ml) jar. Add the fennel seeds and bay leaf. Add enough hot brine to fill the jar and seal with the lid. Cool to room temperature, then refrigerate overnight before using. The beets will keep in the refrigerator for up to 2 weeks.

PICKLED CARROTS

MAKES 1 QUART (960 ML)

1 pound (455 g) carrots, well scrubbed
4 garlic cloves, smashed
4 thyme sprigs
1 teaspoon coriander seeds
1 teaspoon mustard seeds
Basic Pickle Brine (see above), hot

Trim the carrots, leaving a ½-inch (13 mm) nubbin of greens on each carrot. With larger carrots, peel and cut them into sticks. Place the carrots in a 1-quart (960 ml) jar. Add the garlic, thyme, coriander seeds, and mustard seeds to the jar. Add enough hot brine to fill the jar and seal with the lid. Cool to room temperature, then refrigerate overnight before using. The carrots will keep in the refrigerator for up to 2 weeks.

PICKLED CAULIFLOWER

MAKES 1 QUART (960 ML)

1 pound (455 g) cauliflower, cut into uniform bite-size pieces
4 garlic cloves, smashed
½ teaspoon mustard seeds
½ teaspoon whole black peppercorns
¼ teaspoon red pepper flakes
Basic Pickle Brine (page 311), hot

Place the cauliflower in a 1-quart (960 ml) jar. Add the garlic, mustard seeds, peppercorns, and pepper flakes. Add enough hot brine to fill the jar and seal with the lid. Cool to room temperature, then refrigerate overnight before using. The cauliflower will keep in the refrigerator for up to 2 weeks.

PICKLED CELERY

MAKES 1 PINT (480 ML)

8 ounces (225 g) celery ribs, trimmed
4 dill sprigs
½ teaspoons whole black peppercorns
¼ teaspoon red pepper flakes
Basic Pickle Brine (page 311), hot

Slice the celery on an angle into ¼-inch-thick (6 mm) slices. Transfer the celery to a 1-pint (480 ml) jar and add the dill, peppercorns, and pepper flakes. Add enough hot brine to fill the jar and seal with the lid. Cool to room temperature, then refrigerate overnight before using. The celery will keep in the refrigerator for up to 2 weeks.

PICKLED CUCUMBERS

MAKES 1 QUART (960 ML)

1 pound (455 g) cucumbers (any kind)
4 dill sprigs
½ teaspoon mustard seeds
Basic Pickle Brine (page 311), chilled

Slice large cucumbers into spears or rounds; smaller cucumbers can be left whole. Place the cucumbers in a 1-quart (960 ml) jar. Add the dill and mustard seeds. Add enough chilled brine to fill the jar, seal with the lid, and refrigerate for up to 2 weeks.

PICKLED BABY FENNEL

MAKES 1 QUART (960 ML)

1 pound (455 g) baby fennel
Zest of 1 lemon, peeled off in ½-inch (13 mm) strips with a vegetable peeler
½ teaspoon fennel seeds
½ teaspoon whole black peppercorns
Basic Pickle Brine (page 311), hot

Slice the fennel bulbs in half lengthwise. Using a mandoline or a knife, slice the fennel halves into ¼-inch (6 mm) slices. Place the fennel slices in a 1-quart (960 ml) jar and add the lemon zest, fennel seeds, and peppercorns.

aragosta
GOOSE COVE

Add enough hot brine to fill the jar and seal with the lid. Cool to room temperature, then refrigerate overnight before using. The fennel will keep in the refrigerator for up to 2 weeks.

PICKLED STRING BEANS

MAKES 1 QUART (960 ML)

We call these dilly beans in Maine.

1 pound (455 g) string beans, stem ends trimmed
4 dill sprigs
½ teaspoon mustard seeds
¼ teaspoon red pepper flakes
Basic Pickle Brine (page 311), hot

Place the beans in a 1-quart (960 ml) jar. Add the dill, mustard seeds, and pepper flakes. Add enough hot brine to fill the jar and seal with the lid. Cool to room temperature, then refrigerate overnight before using. The string beans will keep in the refrigerator for up to 2 weeks.

PICKLED FIDDLEHEADS

MAKES 1 QUART (960 ML)

Kosher salt
1 pound (455 g) fiddlehead ferns
4 garlic cloves, smashed
1 teaspoon mustard seeds
½ teaspoon whole black peppercorns
Basic Pickle Brine (page 311), hot

1. Set up a large bowl of equal parts ice and water and set it near the stove. In a medium saucepan, bring 2 quarts (1.92 L) liberally salted water to a rolling boil.

2. Wash the fiddleheads well in cold water to remove the papery chaff and trim away any brown ends. Blanch the fiddleheads in the boiling water for 2 minutes, then immediately shock them in the ice water so they stay bright green and crispy.

3. Drain the fiddleheads and transfer them to a 1-quart (960 ml) jar. Add the garlic, mustard seeds, and peppercorns. Add enough hot brine to fill the jar and seal with the lid. Cool to room temperature, then refrigerate overnight before using. The fiddleheads will keep in the refrigerator for up to 2 weeks.

PICKLED GARLIC SCAPES

MAKES 1 QUART (960 ML)

8 ounces (225 g) garlic scapes (about 20, depending on size)
1 teaspoon mustard seeds
1 teaspoon whole black peppercorns
Basic Pickle Brine (page 311), hot

Wash and trim the garlic scapes, removing the papery tops so that only the round lighter green bulb remains. You can keep the scapes in their natural curly state or slice them so that they will stand up in the jar, whichever you prefer. Transfer the scapes to a 1-quart

(960 ml) jar and add the mustard seeds and peppercorns. Add enough hot brine to fill the jar and seal with the lid. Cool to room temperature, then refrigerate overnight before using. The garlic scapes will keep in the refrigerator for up to 2 weeks.

NOTE: If you get scapes with the buds still on them, they are beautiful and delicious additions to the pickle.

PICKLED PEPPERS

MAKES 1 QUART (960 ML)

1 pound peppers (see Note)
2 garlic cloves, smashed
½ teaspoon whole black peppercorns
Basic Pickle Brine (page 311), hot

For small spicy peppers, thinly slice them crosswise into ¼-inch (6 mm) rounds, removing the seeds if you want the pickles to be milder. Larger peppers should be sliced into strips about ¼ inch (6 mm) wide. Transfer the peppers to a 1-quart (960 ml) jar and add the garlic and peppercorns. Add enough hot brine to fill the jar and seal with the lid. Cool to room temperature, then refrigerate overnight before using. The peppers will keep in the refrigerator for up to 2 weeks.

NOTE: Any kind of pepper can be pickled, but smaller varieties such as banana peppers and jalapeños are my favorites.

PICKLED DAIKON RADISH

MAKES 1 PINT (480 ML)

8 ounces (250 g) daikon radish, scrubbed
½ teaspoon mustard seeds
½ teaspoon whole black peppercorns
Basic Pickle Brine (page 311), hot

Using a mandoline or a knife, thinly slice the daikon lengthwise into ¼-inch-thick (6 mm) slices, leaving ¼ inch (6 mm) of green stem for an attractive look. Transfer the daikon to a 1-pint (480 ml) jar and add the mustard seeds and peppercorns. Add enough hot brine to fill the jar and seal with the lid. Cool to room temperature, then refrigerate overnight before using. The daikon radish will keep in the refrigerator for up to 2 weeks.

PICKLED RAMPS

MAKES 1 PINT (480 ML)

12 ounces (340 g) ramps (24 to 48 ramps, depending on size)
½ teaspoon coriander seeds
½ teaspoon whole black peppercorns
¼ teaspoon red pepper flakes
Basic Pickle Brine (page 311), hot

Wash and clean the ramps, removing the roots and leaves—you are only pickling the bottom part of each ramp. Remove the outer layer of the ramps, the same way you would peel a scallion or leek. Make sure to remove all the soil and grit. Transfer the ramps to a

1-pint (480 ml) jar. Add the coriander seeds, peppercorns, and pepper flakes. Add enough hot brine to fill the jar and seal with the lid. Cool to room temperature, then refrigerate overnight before using. The ramps will keep in the refrigerator for up to 2 weeks.

PICKLED RED ONIONS OR SHALLOTS

MAKES 1 PINT (480 ML)

8 ounces (225 g) red onion or shallots
½ teaspoon mustard seeds
½ teaspoon whole black peppercorns
Basic Pickle Brine (page 311), hot

Using a mandoline or a knife, thinly slice the onion or shallots. Place the sliced onion or shallots in a 1-pint (480 ml) jar. Add the mustard seeds and peppercorns. Add enough hot brine to fill the jar and seal with the lid. Cool to room temperature, then refrigerate overnight before using. The onions or shallots will keep in the refrigerator for up to 2 weeks.

PICKLED HAKUREI TURNIPS

MAKES 1 PINT (480 ML)

Also known as baby turnips, Hakurei are the only members of the turnip family that don't need to be cooked in order to be eaten. When pickled, they are crunchy and mild.

½ pound (225 g) Hakurei turnips, scrubbed but unpeeled
1 bay leaf
½ teaspoon mustard seeds
½ teaspoon whole black peppercorns
Basic Pickle Brine (page 311), hot

Using a mandoline or a knife, cut the turnips lengthwise into ¼-inch-thick (6 mm) slices. You'll want to leave ¼ inch (6 mm) of the green top. You can also cut the turnips into small wedges. Transfer the turnips to a 1-pint (480 ml) jar. Add the bay leaf, mustard seeds, and peppercorns. Add enough hot brine to fill the jar and seal with the lid. Cool to room temperature, then refrigerate overnight before using. The turnips will keep in the refrigerator for up to 2 weeks.

PICKLED ZUCCHINI OR SUMMER SQUASH

MAKES 1 QUART (960 ML)

1 pound (455 g) zucchini or summer squash, cut into ¼-inch-thick (6 mm) rounds
4 garlic cloves, smashed
½ teaspoon coriander seeds
½ teaspoon whole black peppercorns
¼ teaspoon red pepper flakes
Basic Pickle Brine (page 311), chilled

Place the squash in a 1-quart (960 ml) jar. Add the garlic, coriander seeds, peppercorns, and pepper flakes. Add enough chilled brine to fill the jar, seal with the lid, and refrigerate for up to 2 weeks.

PICKLED SHIMEJI MUSHROOMS

MAKES 1 PINT (480 ML)

A brine featuring a mix of Asian ingredients and spices makes for a unique mushroom pickle that can be at home on a cheese plate or tossed in a green salad.

12 ounces (345 g) shimeji mushrooms, bottoms trimmed and evened
⅓ cup (80 ml) tamari
⅓ cup (80 ml) rice vinegar
3 tablespoons mirin
2 cinnamon sticks
2 whole star anise
1 tablespoon whole black peppercorns
2 whole cloves

1. Place the mushrooms in a large heatproof bowl.

2. In a nonreactive saucepan, combine the tamari, vinegar, mirin, cinnamon sticks, star anise, peppercorns, and cloves. Cook over medium heat, stirring often, until the liquid just begins to bubble. Pour the hot marinade over the mushrooms and gently stir with a wooden spoon or spatula. The hot liquid will infuse and very lightly cook the delicate mushrooms. While the mushrooms are still warm but cool enough to handle, gently massage them in the liquid to help the flavors penetrate the mushrooms. Set aside to cool for 1 hour.

3. Transfer the mushrooms and liquid to a 1-pint (480 ml) jar, seal with the lid, and refrigerate. The pickled mushrooms will keep for about 1 month.

Resources

Unless otherwise noted, whatever ingredients your local markets or online purveyors have in stock will work fine for all the recipes in this book. For Maine-based recommendations, those can often be found online if you're not in Maine. Here are some of my particular favorites from Maine's farmers and fishers and others. Following the ingredients are some of my favorite places to visit for your next trip to Maine.

Ingredients and Equipment

CLAM JUICE

Bar Harbor Foods
barharborfoods.com

FARMS AND FARM STANDS

5 Star Orchard
5starorchard.com
Apples, apple cider, peaches, plums, and pears.

Carding Brook Farm
cardingbrookfarm.com
A 200-year-old saltwater farm in Brooklin offering fruits and vegetables.

Deer Isle Farmers' Market & Artists' Market
20 Church Street
Farmers' market: Every Wednesday, 9:30 a.m. to 11:30 a.m., May to October.
Artists' market: Every Thursday, 10 a.m. to 2 p.m., May to October.

Fine Line Farm
finelinefarmmaine.com
They grow some crops exclusively for Aragosta.

Four Season Farm
fourseasonfarm.com
Produce and flowers. Created by Eliot Coleman and Barbara Damrosch, the godparents of modern organic gardening. They helped me get started with my first restaurant and have been dear friends and guides ever since.

Stonington Farmers' Market
43 School Street
Every Friday, 10 a.m. to 12 p.m., May to October.

Yellow Birch Farm
yellowbirchfarm.com
This farmstead produces cheese, gelatos, soap, fruits, and vegetables, plus they

have the Greene Ziner Gallery of art and ceramics (they make my bowls and plates, and their work is in the Smithsonian).

FRESH AND SMOKED SEAFOOD

Coldwater Seafood
coldwaterseafoodmaine.com

FLOURS AND BEANS

Maine Grains
mainegrains.com

JAMS, JELLIES, AND CHUTNEYS

Nervous Nellie's Jams and Jellies
nervousnellies.com

LOBSTER, PEEKYTOE CRAB, AND MUSSELS

Greenhead Lobster
greenheadlobster.com

MUSHROOMS

Down East Mushrooms
downeastmushrooms.com

OUTDOOR EQUIPMENT

Yeti Skillets and Dutch Ovens
yeti.com
I love using cast iron because it heats so evenly and has a great old-timey feel. In my experience, Yeti makes the best modern cast-iron cookware.

OYSTERS

Deer Isle Oyster Company
deerisleoysterco.com

Fish Creek Oysters
fishcreekoysters.com

SUGAR KELP AND DULSE

Maine Coast Sea Vegetables
seaveg.com

WILD MAINE BLUEBERRIES

Allen's Wild Blueberries
allenswild.com

Blue-Zee Farm
bluezeefarm.com

Things to Do and See on Deer Isle and the Blue Hill Peninsula

There are winding country roads, picturesque farms and houses, seaside and forest rambles, and scenic views everywhere on Deer Isle and the Blue Hill Peninsula. Here are a few of my favorite places.

Stonington
With its flotilla of fishing boats that make it the largest seafood port in Maine, Stonington is a thoroughly charming village of clapboard homes and small shops. During the growing season, the farmers' market offers many of the same products used in Aragosta's recipes. A ferry can take you to Isle au Haut, where you can hike, bike, or just hang out. If you'd like a trip on the water, **Good Tide Tours** plies the local waters in an old-timey lobster boat with Captain Walker Collin at the helm (goodtidetours.com).

ARTS AND ARTISANS

Deer Isle and the Blue Hill Peninsula have long been an attraction for some of America's greatest artists. Whether you are coming to learn or to buy, there is much to see here.

Haystack Mountain School of Crafts
Deer Isle
haystack-mtn.org
Located on a stunning spit of land, the 45-acre campus of this artisans' mecca is listed on the National Register of Historic Places. The *New York Times*

named the wooden complex one of the most significant architectural works of the past 25 years. Artisans working in wood, fabrics, metal, and ceramics come to Haystack for workshops and studio residencies. Even if you are not a craftsperson, you can enjoy tours of the campus, studio visits, and auctions. Reserve your visit online.

The Turtle Gallery
61 North Deer Isle Road
Deer Isle
theturtlegallery.com
Featuring the works of Deer Isle artists and artisans.

Makers' Market
47 Caterpillar Hill Road
Sedgwick
makersmarketmaine.com
Year-round craft and studio shop on the Blue Hill Peninsula offering local art, gifts, provisions, beer, and wine.

Jud Hartmann Gallery
79 Main Street
Blue Hill
judhartmanngallery.com
Extraordinary wooden sculptures of Native Americans of the Northeast.

Carolyn Walton Gallery
131 North Deer Isle Road
Deer Isle
carolynwalton.com
Beautiful paintings of Maine scenes by a renowned Deer Isle artist.

Holley Mead, Goose Chase Quilts
Seamark Gallery
11 Church Street
Deer Isle
holleymead.com
Quilts, pillows, and wall hangings inspired by scenes of Maine.

WALKS, TRAILS, AND PARKS

There are many walks and trails on Deer Isle and the Blue Hill Peninsula. These are some of my favorites. The Island Heritage Trust has published a complete list for Deer Isle; visit islandheritagetrust.org/visit-a-preserve.

Barred Island Preserve
Deer Isle
This trail, just outside Goose Cove, is an easy walk through the forest, and at low tide, you can walk across the sand spit that connects the island to Deer Isle.

Sand Beach
Deer Isle
If you travel down any road on Deer Isle that leads to the western shore, you are guaranteed a lovely sunset over Penobscot Bay and the mainland across the water. Sand Beach is just outside Stonington and easily accessible.

Settlement Quarry
Oceanville Road
Deer Isle
Huge granite blocks that helped build New York City's George Washington, Williamsburg, and Triborough bridges were carved out of this rocky formation. Now it is a preserve with nearly 2 miles of trails and panoramic views of Isle au Haut.

Caterpillar Hill
Rte. 175
Sedgwick
You will pass Caterpillar Hill and its overlook of Penobscot Bay shortly after entering the Blue Hill Peninsula. The bay lies to your right, and on your left is a meadow where retreating glaciers of the last ice age thoughtfully deposited white and gray boulders for scenic effect.

Holbrook Island Sanctuary
Cape Rozier Road
Brooksville
One of many beautiful parks and trails along the coast of the Blue Hill Peninsula. It's a great spot for a picnic, and they have some nice tables set up to overlook Penobscot Bay. One of the treats on the way there is Condon's Garage, which looks just the same as it did in Robert McCloskey's timeless children's book *One Morning in Maine*.

Lookout Rock
Brooksville
mcht.org/preserve/lookout-rock
A short, steep walk with a great payoff: panoramic views of Eggemoggin Reach, Penobscot Bay, and beyond.

Blue Hill Mountain Trail
bluehillheritagetrust.org/blue-hill-mountain
A relatively easy trail with some of the most thrilling views.

A Few of My Favorite Places for a Down-Home Meal, Fine Dining, Pastry, and Coffee

44 North
Deer Isle Village and Stonington
44northcoffee.com
Serves delicious custom-roasted drip coffee and pastries. Every day a different local bakery provides breads and pastries, both sweet and savory.

Bagaduce Lunch
Penobscot
No trip to coastal Maine is complete without some fried clams, lobster rolls, French fries, and coleslaw. Located on the Blue Hill Peninsula in nearby Brooksville, this James Beard Award winner perches above tidal narrows in the Bagaduce River. The menu hasn't changed since opening day in 1946. Neither has the old-timey building and its wooden picnic tables in the shady backyard.

Fish Net
Blue Hill
An informal longtime favorite for lobster, fried seafood, and chowders.

LDI Lobster
Little Deer Isle
Located right by the bridge over Eggemoggin Reach, it's great for old-timey Maine seafood.

The Pilgrim's Inn
20 Main Street
Deer Isle
pilgrimsinn.com/dine
Terrific and innovative dining in the heart of Deer Isle Village.

Tinder Hearth
Brooksville
tinderhearth.com
Located in a picturesque old barn, and it has a picnic grove for outdoor dining. This bakery by day and pizzeria by night turns out pastries and pizzas that are as good as any you will find in a metropolitan food capital. On Friday night, Abby Barrows offers oysters on the half shell. You'll need to book reservations for pizza and oyster nights.

AND . . . WHERE YOU CAN FIND ME:

Aragosta
300 Goose Cove Road
Deer Isle
aragostamaine.com

Acknowledgments

For my love of cooking and gardening and their loving support, my mom and dad, Kevin and Terri Finigan. Eliot Coleman, Barbara Damrosch, George Semler, and Donald Sussman for believing in me and Aragosta. Liam Lawford for the many years of dedication to Aragosta. Dan Marchese, Matt Adrian, Cameron Coyle, Kristen Rollins, Tyler Wardwell, and Rosy Whitney for being there 25/7. Sarah Pebworth and Butch Smith for getting me started as a chef. Krishna Fitzpatrick for her years of friendship and her artistry. Judy Pray for her guiding hand, Suet Chong for her lovely aesthetic, and the team at Artisan, including Lia Ronnen, Hillary Leary, Donna Brown, Brooke Beckmann, and Theresa Collier. Paul Bresnick and David Black for putting Peter and me and Artisan together. William Hereford for his spirit and his photos. Melinda Kaminsky for reading everything over and over. Luke Hartmann for our years together, believing in making Aragosta possible, and our beautiful children. Matt Spector for the time and care he put into this book. Kathleen Hackett for her well-learned Maine-ness. For IRL recipe tests, Joe McCarthy, Pam Maffei McCarthy, Ellen Foote, Steve Hindy, Lynn Boulger, Tim Garrity, Sherry Streeter, Jon Wilson, Whitney Harvey, Sam Koh, Lily Kaminsky, Martha Spector, Shawn Riley, and Ben Jardine. Annie Taylor Gray for her Deer Isle knowledge. Finally, Teddy and Tootsie, the world's best bulldogs.

Index

Page numbers in *italics* refer to photographs.

About the Authors

DEVIN FINIGAN grew up in the Green Mountains of Vermont, inheriting her love of cooking from her dad, who was a chef at a fine dining restaurant, and her passion for gardening from her mom. On a chance visit as a teenager to Deer Isle, Maine, she decided to give up her dream of becoming an Olympic snowboarder and make her life on this picturesque Maine island.

Working her way up through the kitchens of the Blue Hill Peninsula, in 2010 Devin became the head chef at the Blue Hill Inn. There, her talent as a chef and restaurateur set her on a path to open her own restaurant focused on prime local ingredients and elegant, innovative cuisine.

Devin founded her restaurant, Aragosta, in 2013, in a small space in Stonington, the main town on Deer Isle. Over the following six years, she developed her unique vision for modern fine dining with a pronounced Maine accent, honing her skills as stagiaire in the celebrated kitchens of The French Laundry, Per Se, Blue Hill at Stone Barns, and SingleThread. In 2019, she moved her restaurant and two daughters to a stunning 22-acre forest overlooking Goose Cove. In 2024, *Food & Wine* recognized Aragosta as the number two restaurant in America, and in 2025, *Food & Wine* named it the number two hotel for food and drink.

PETER KAMINSKY has written nineteen cookbooks, including *Seven Fires* with Francis Mallmann, *The Elements of Taste* with Gray Kunz, and *Ultimate Tailgating* with John Madden. He was *New York* magazine's Underground Gourmet for four years, and his food writing has appeared frequently in *Food & Wine* as well as the food section of the *New York Times*. He is among America's foremost flyfishing authors and was the leading contributor to the *New York Times* Outdoors column for thirty-five years. He is the author of *Pig Perfect: Encounters with Remarkable Swine*; *Culinary Intelligence: The Art of Eating Healthy (and Really Well)*; *The Moon Pulled Up an Acre of Bass*; and *The Zen of Flyfishing*. His television credits include creator and executive producer of *The Mark Twain Prize for American Humor* and *The Library of Congress Gershwin Prize for Popular Song*. He lives in Brooklyn, New York.